AF322714

Chinese Mythology for Teens

Ancient China's Mystical World of Dragons, Emperors, and Mythical Beings

© Copyright 2026 - All rights reserved.

The content contained within this book may not be reproduced, duplicated, or transmitted without direct written permission from the author or the publisher.

Under no circumstances will any blame or legal responsibility be held against the publisher, or author, for any damages, reparation, or monetary loss due to the information contained within this book, either directly or indirectly.

Legal Notice:

This book is copyright protected. It is only for personal use. You cannot amend, distribute, sell, use, quote, or paraphrase any part, or the content within this book, without the consent of the author or publisher.

Disclaimer Notice:

Please note the information contained within this document is for educational and entertainment purposes only. All effort has been executed to present accurate, up-to-date, reliable, and complete information. No warranties of any kind are declared or implied. Readers acknowledge that the author is not engaging in the rendering of legal, financial, medical, or professional advice. The content within this book has been derived from various sources. Please consult a licensed professional before attempting any techniques outlined in this book.

By reading this document, the reader agrees that under no circumstances is the author responsible for any losses, direct or indirect, that are incurred as a result of the use of the information contained within this document, including, but not limited to, errors, omissions, or inaccuracies.

Free limited time bonus

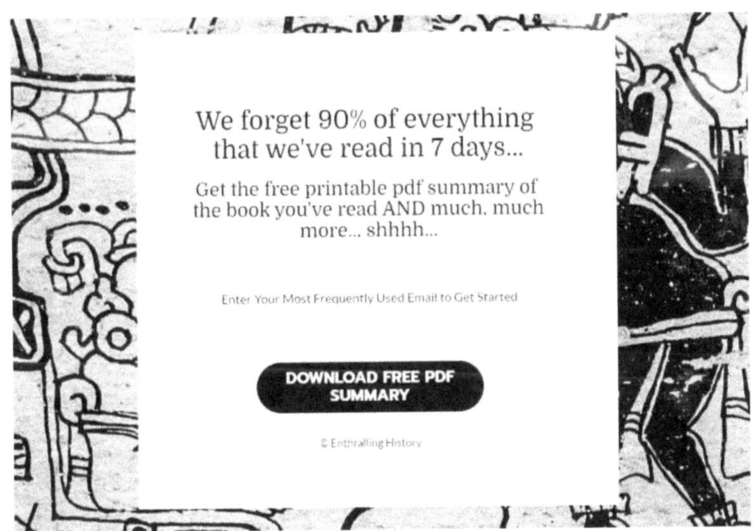

Stop for a moment. We have a free bonus set up for you. The problem is this: we forget 90% of everything that we read after 7 days. Crazy fact, right? Here's the solution: we've created a printable, 1-page pdf summary for this book that you're reading now. All you have to do to get your free pdf summary is to go to the following website:

https://livetolearn.lpages.co/enthrallinghistory/

Or, Scan the QR code!

Once you do, it will be intuitive. Enjoy, and thank you!

Table of Contents

INTRODUCTION 1

CRASH COURSE IN PRONOUNCING PINYIN 3

CHAPTER 1: THE CREATION COSMOS: PANGU AND THE BIRTH OF THE WORLD 5

CHAPTER 2: THE DESCENT OF THE GODDESS: NUWA'S GIFT TO HUMANITY 17

CHAPTER 3: JOURNEY TO IMMORTALITY: THE QUEST OF THE EIGHT IMMORTALS 28

CHAPTER 4: THE EMPEROR'S SECRET: THE ELIXIR OF LIFE...................41

CHAPTER 5: THE WEAVER AND THE COWHERD: A LOVE STORY WRITTEN IN THE STARS 51

CHAPTER 6: THE SUN CHASER: THE ENDURANCE OF HOU YI 60

CHAPTER 7: THE DRAGON'S PEARL: RULERS OF RIVERS AND SEAS 67

CHAPTER 8: THE MONKEY KING'S REBELLION: JOURNEY TO THE WEST 77

CHAPTER 9: THE LANTERN FESTIVAL: A TALE OF REUNION AND LIGHT 88

CHAPTER 10: THE IMMORTAL PEACH: THE BANQUET OF THE GODS 98

HERE'S ANOTHER BOOK BY ENTHRALLING HISTORY THAT YOU MIGHT LIKE...107

FREE LIMITED TIME BONUS...108

BIBLIOGRAPHY 109

IMAGE SOURCES 111

Introduction

Dragons, heroes, monsters, gods, and an impish Monkey King—Chinese mythology has it all! Who broke the sky and who fixed it? How did Yu the Engineer end the Great Flood? What happened when a goddess fell in love with a cowherd? Who saved the day when ten suns scorched the Earth? Could a person become immortal? Whose rabbit is on the moon? This book unravels these stories and much more.

People, animals, and mythical creatures all appear in Chinese mythology. These myths explain how the world began and unravel the relationship between people and supernatural beings. The stories help decode life's mysteries, revealing how the ancient Chinese perceived the world around them. These perceptions continue to shape the Chinese worldview today and foster a shared identity.

These rich and diverse stories involve humble people, emperors, princesses, immortals, and divine beings. Some myths feature real people around whom legends formed. A few stories contradict other tales, as they arose in different parts of China or across different eras. Today, during China's annual festivals, children gather to hear these stories. Myths explain Moon Day, the Dragon Boat Festival, and other holidays in the Chinese calendar. Chinese television replays these myths, with the exploits of the mischievous Monkey King always a favorite.

China's mythology opens a window into ancient culture. For nearly four thousand years, China experienced many dynasties, during which one family ruled parts or all of the country. The "Mandate of Heaven" was Heaven's blessing over a righteous and wise ruling family. If an emperor became foolish or evil, his family line lost Heaven's Mandate, and another clan rose to power. As China changed over the millennia, its mythology evolved as new religions and philosophies, notably Taoism, Confucianism, and Buddhism, emerged.

Now, let's take a look at how the ancient Chinese believed their world began—with an egg.

Crash Course in Pronouncing Pinyin

Most of us achieved basic reading skills by the end of first grade. Can you imagine, instead of learning 26 letters, you had to learn the meaning and sounds of 1,600 characters by the end of second grade? That is the reality for Chinese children. English is **phonetic**, meaning its letters represent sounds. Chinese is **logographic**, meaning each symbol (or character) stands for a word or part of a word.

The good news is that you do not have to learn complicated characters to read the Chinese names and common Chinese expressions in this book. Chinese has a second written language called **Pinyin**, which is based on sounds, as in English. It uses the same twenty-six letters used in English.

Chinese people use Pinyin for typing and texting. Pinyin is also invaluable for *laowai* (foreigners) to read Chinese without having to memorize thousands of characters. This quick guide to pronouncing Pinyin will help you sound out most Chinese words. (Do not worry about tone markings; this book does not use them.)

Consonants

The pronunciation of the consonants b, d, f, g, h, j, k, l, m, n, p, s, and t is basically the same as in English. Here are the ones that are different.

- "Q" sounds like the English "ch" (like in church). The word "Qing" sounds like "cheeng."

- "X" has an "sh" sound (like in shout), so "Xi'an" sounds like "shee ahn."

- "Z" sounds like the "ds" in "ki**ds**."

- "C" sounds like the "ts" in "pa**ts**."

Four Chinese consonant sounds (zh, ch, sh, r) are **retroflex consonants**. You curl the tip of your tongue up and touch the top of your mouth behind your top teeth, slightly hissing as you say the sound.

- "Zh" sounds like the English "j," but it's retroflex. The Chinese word "Zhou" sounds like "Joe" but with your tongue curled back and slightly hissing.

- "Ch" sounds like our "ch" but retroflex, slightly hissing. The Chinese name "Chu" sounds like "chew" but with your tongue curled back and slightly hissing.

- "Sh" is like our "sh" but retroflex. The Chinese name "Shou" sounds like "show" but retroflex.

- "R" is like the English "r" but retroflex.

Vowels

- "A" sounds like the "ah" in "mama."

- "O" sounds like the "o" in "flow."

- "E" sounds like the short "e" in "send."

- "I" sounds like the long "e" in "meet" ("Pinyin" sounds like "peen yeen").

- "U" sounds like the "oo" sound in "mood."

Common Vowel Blends

- "Ai" sounds like the long English "i" in "sight."

- "Ao" sounds like "ow" in "cow."

- "Ou" sounds like the English "oh."

- "Ei" sounds like the "ay" sound in "bay" (Beijing is pronounced "bay jeeng").

Chapter 1: The Creation Cosmos: Pangu and the Birth of the World

This chapter and the next unwrap China's creation myths. These stories lay the groundwork for Chinese mythology and explain why the values of harmony and interconnectedness are central to Chinese culture. They provide a rich backdrop for appreciating the depth of China's ancient heritage.

Pangu and the Primordial Egg

Pangu's story explains how the universe began. A government official and historian named Xu Zheng wrote the creation myth in the Eastern Wu dynasty (222–280 CE). However, it may have been a legend passed down by word of mouth for generations.

In the beginning, there was only darkness, emptiness, and spiraling chaos. The twisting turmoil formed a primeval egg, holding all the universe in its small space. **Yin and Yang** were inside the egg: two opposite forces that constantly struggled against each other except on rare occasions when they achieved harmony and balance. Yin represented light and movement, and Yang represented darkness and rest. Yin was day, and Yang was night.

Yin and Yang violently wrestled for a very long time. It is not known how long since time could not yet be measured. Finally, they achieved harmony and equality for the first time. When they did, a fat, hairy, horned dwarf formed inside the egg. For a countless amount of time, he slept as his body developed. His name was Pangu. Somehow, when he awakened from his long slumber, he had an ax in his hand. He swung the ax, splitting Yin and Yang, and broke the egg. Pangu emerged from the egg, and the rest of the universe spilled out after him.

Pangu swung his ax again, splitting the universe in two, forming Earth and sky. At first, the sky was only a foot or two above Earth. Pangu pushed the sky up, away from Earth. The harder he pushed, the higher the sky rose. Pangu stretched out as he pushed the sky away from Earth until he transformed from a fat dwarf into an impressive giant.

Pangu [1]

For eighteen thousand years, Pangu held up the sky. Finally, he died. His final breath transformed into the clouds and wind. The sun and moon formed from his eyes, and his blood became the rivers coursing through the soil, formed by his muscles. His arms and legs transformed into the four pillars (or sacred mountains) that held up the sky. Pangu's teeth and bones formed various metals and rocks. His long, shaggy hair became trees and plants.

Pangu's story reflects the Chinese moral values of balance, diligence, and sacrifice. The opposing forces of Yin and Yang had to come into balance for creation to begin. One of China's values is the sacrifice of the individual for the family's greater good. In Pangu's case, his "family" was humanity. People had not yet been created, but the sacrifice of Pangu's body created the ideal habitat for them. His perseverance in holding up the sky models the Chinese values of hard work and diligence. The Chinese see time as cyclical rather than proceeding in a straight line. Pangu's death was not the end but the beginning of a new form of existence.

Oracle Bones and Shangdi, China's First God

Pangu's story of creation does not mention a god. Pangu was a Taoist legend, and Taoism began as a philosophy and later evolved into a religion with deities. The Chinese people eventually began worshiping Pangu as a god, as they often did with illustrious ancestors.

Did the ancient Chinese believe in a creator god? Yes, they did. His name was **Shangdi**, and the Chinese people wrote his name on **oracle bones** about 1,400 years before Xu Zheng wrote Pangu's story.

What were oracle bones? Chinese traditional medicine has used "dinosaur bones" (which they call "dragon bones") for millennia. A little over a century ago, a Chinese man named Wang Yirong bought some "dragon bone" medicine when he had malaria. Usually, the pharmacist ground up the bones, but this time, they came in chunks. Wang Yirong noticed writing on the bones.

Oracle bones from the Shang dynasty [2]

Fortunately, he was a scholar and investigated the bones further. The so-called dragon bones were actually from water buffalo and oxen. Still, they were priceless. The bones were about 3,500 years old and represented China's first writing, which began in the Shang dynasty (1600–1046 BCE). Wang Yirong and his associates scoured Chinese pharmacies, buying all the bones they could find. Amazingly, around fifty thousand of these bones have survived.

Why did the Shang dynasty Chinese write on bones? They used them for fortune-telling. The king—or just about anyone else—could consult an **oracle** (a priest or a fortune teller) with a question about the future. The seer would write his question on one side of a large bone. On the other side, he drilled little holes, then stuck a red-hot skewer into the holes until the bone cracked. The way it cracked gave the answer to the question in this practice, which is called **pyro-osteomancy**.

The Chinese writing system has evolved since the Shang dynasty, but the basics have remained. Modern-day Chinese scholars can interpret the pictographs and symbols written on the oracle bones. China's early writing opened a window into its belief system. The god Shangdi's name was everywhere. The Chinese of that era consulted him about the future. Other writings declared their devotion to Shangdi as the ultimate spiritual power. Sometimes, they consulted their ancestral spirits on the oracle bones, asking them to plead with Shangdi.

Who was Shangdi? "Shang" means "superior," "preceding," or "topmost." "Di" means "emperor" or "god." He was the first and highest god, the primordial emperor of Heaven. The "Border Sacrifice" began in the Shang dynasty or possibly even in the shadowy Xia dynasty (2070–1600 BCE) that preceded it. The emperor annually sacrificed a sheep or bull to Shangdi at Mount Tai, China's southern border (and later in Beijing), proclaiming, "Of old, in the beginning, there was the great chaos, without form and dark. The five elements [planets] had not begun to revolve, nor the sun and moon to shine. You, O Spiritual Sovereign, first divided the grosser parts from the purer. You made Heaven. You made Earth. You made man. All things with their reproducing power got their being."[i]

The Four Sacred Beasts

Confucian scholars wrote the *Book of Rites* in the early Han dynasty (206 BCE–220 CE) based on earlier writings that Emperor Qin Shi Huang had burned in 213 BCE. The scholars had either memorized the books or hidden some away. The *Book of Rites* tells about the **Four Sacred Beasts** that assisted with creation. Technically, **Confucianism** was a philosophy based on the teachings of Kong Fuzi or Confucius (551–479 BCE) on how people should live and how government should be run. However, Confucianism included a deep reverence for **Tian** (Heaven), promoted ancestor worship, and coexisted with the diverse spirits and deities of Chinese folk religion.

The Four Sacred Beasts represented the four directions. **Turtle (or Black Tortoise)** was north, **Azure Dragon** was east, **Fenghuang (Phoenix)** was south, and **Qilin (often called the Chinese unicorn)** was west. Xu Zheng did not include the Four Sacred Beasts in his Pangu story, and the Confucian scholars did not include Pangu in the *Book of Rites*. However, as time passed, they merged.

---

[i] James Legge, *The Notions of the Chinese Concerning Gods and Spirits* (Hong Kong Register, 1852), 28.

Phoenix and Azure Dragon on China's state emblem (1913-1928) [3]

The fiery Qilin had a body like a horse and the head and tail of a dragon. If anyone saw the Qilin, it meant either the birth or death of an exceptional emperor or sage. White pottery depicting Fenghuang, the phoenix-like creature, dates to around 5000 BCE and was excavated at the Gaomiao archaeological site in Hunan Province. Ceramic dragon images date to around 5400 BCE in the Xinglongwa culture of northeastern China. The dragon and phoenix together first appeared in Shaanxi Province's Yangshao culture (5000–3000 BCE). In some periods, the Chinese believed the dragon and phoenix were married, representing the emperor and empress.

At creation, the Four Sacred Beasts formed the cosmos. They established five seasons (summer, late summer, fall, winter, and spring). They created Wuxing, the **five elements** (fire, water, wood, earth, and metal). These elements were connected to the five planets that one can see with the naked eye: Mercury, Venus, Mars, Jupiter, and Saturn. (And yes, the ancient Chinese discerned the planets from stars by the way they moved through the sky). The elements interacted with each other and passed through cycles.

Fire represented energy, warmth, and transformation. Water stood for adaptability, nourishment, and the flow of things. Wood represented vitality, growth, and flexibility. Earth was balance, fertility, and stability. Metal was clarity, strength, and transformation. The five elements could either nourish and support the others, or they could destroy. For instance, water causes wood to grow, which fuels fire. Fire's ashes create earth, which contains metal, which carries water. On the other hand, wood (tree roots) digs into the earth. Earth creates dams to stop water. Water puts out fire, fire melts metal, and metal cuts wood.

Bamboo and Turtle

This is a story about a reunion of the Sacred Beasts. It involves Zhuzi, a young teen, whose name meant "Bamboo." Zhuzi's father was the caretaker of the royal tombs of the Liang dynasty (502–557 CE). One of the ancient temples in the complex was the tomb of Prince Xiao Xu, the brother of a Liang emperor. That temple was near Zhuzi's cottage. Although the gates to the temple were always locked, Zhuzi liked to stand outside the gate and peer through the open door of the temple. A huge stone turtle holding a tall pillar on its back interested him. It was dark inside the temple, but the sun shone through the door, so he could see the turtle's dim outline.

"Baba," he once asked his father. "Why does that little temple have a turtle inside it? And why does it have a pillar on its back?"

"Well, it's a kind of memorial, with inscriptions of decrees and important events in the prince's lifetime," his father explained.

"Why a turtle?" asked Zhuzi. "It doesn't seem very royal to me."

"Ah, Zhuzi, remember? The turtle was one of the Four Sacred Beasts. He is a symbol of Earth, longevity, and cosmic stability."

Zhuzi laughed. "Well, I can see why he symbolizes longevity! He must have been there since the beginning of time. He's covered in dust!"

A turtle at Xiao Xu's temple[4]

One day, some dignitaries arrived to visit the tombs. The sedan chairs they rode in captivated Zhuzi. He started to follow the procession, but his father grabbed his arm, hissing, "Don't follow them like that! They'll think you're a beggar!"

His father hurried off to unlock the temples. Zhuzi watched from the doorway of the cottage as the group visited the nearby temple, then continued on their way.

"Ha! Father forgot to lock Prince Xiao Xu's temple! Now is my chance to get a closer look at that turtle!"

He peered down the road and smiled. His father was out of sight. Quickly, Zhuzi hurried to the temple, slipped through the open gate, and went toward the temple. But as he stepped through the door, his foot caught on the threshold, and he fell flat on his face. He lay there for a moment, slightly stunned. Then, the ancient dust on the floor made him sneeze. Suddenly, he heard something move. Was it inside or outside? Maybe someone was coming! Zhuzi quickly crawled under the stone turtle. Suddenly, he heard a voice!

"Stop moving around! You're sending up a cloud of dust. It's choking me."

Who was talking? Could it be the turtle?

"Are you alive?" Zhuzi whispered.

"I have been alive since the world began! Now, stop wriggling around! You're sending dust everywhere!"

"Dui bu qi!" ("I'm sorry!") Zhuzi apologized, giving the turtle a respectful *gongshou* salute with his left hand covering his right fist.

"*Mei guanxi.*" ("It's okay.") "Why are you in here?"

"I have looked at you many times from outside the gate, but I always wanted to see you up close."

"Really?" The turtle smiled. "Everyone who comes in here reads the writing on the pillar but barely glances at me. No one knows I'm the son of one of the Four Sacred Beasts!"

"For real?" Zhuzi's jaw dropped in astonishment. "Your father helped create the seasons and elements?"

"Actually, it was my grandfather. But it's all the same, isn't it?"

Zhuzi stared at the turtle in astonishment.

"Now, get moving!" commanded the turtle. "Go out there and close that gate before your father gets back and sees it. He'll lock both of us inside!"

Zhuzi ran out into the courtyard, careful not to trip over the raised threshold, and closed the gate. Then he hurried back into the temple.

The turtle sighed. "My back hurts! I've been holding this pillar on my back for over a hundred years! It's time to escape!"

Zhuzi gasped. "Oh, please! Don't leave! If you go missing, my father will be executed for not locking the gate!"

"Oh, I have a plan!" the turtle chuckled. "Once I'm gone, quietly get your father's keys, lock the gate, and put the keys back. It will be wonderful! Everyone knows I'm too heavy to pick up. No one will blame your father. They will think the gods made me disappear! Thousands of pilgrims will come visit my little temple!"

Zhuzi nodded, smiling. But then a tear trickled down his cheek. "I'll miss you!"

"Well, why don't you come with me? We'll go on an adventure! I'll have you back home before sunset!"

"Hao de!" ("Okay!") Zhuzi grinned. But then he frowned. "How will you get out the door with that pillar on your back? You won't fit!"

"Ah! I've been here for a long time thinking about how to do that. I think as I walk through the doorway, the pillar will bump the lintel over the door and slide off my back to the floor."

What actually happened was that when the turtle clambered over the threshold, the pillar swayed. When it hit the lintel, the pillar fell over backward, slammed into the ground, and crumbled into pieces. "Oh, no!" Zhuzi gasped. "I hope my father didn't hear that!"

They waited a few minutes, but no one came running. "Ah, my father must still be at the tombs then."

He followed the giant turtle as it crawled slowly across the courtyard and through the gate.

"Are we going very far?" Zhuzi asked. "You're a slow walker!"

"Yes, I don't walk much, you see," the turtle answered. "Certainly not recently! I've been stuck inside that temple! To answer your question, we are going to where the world began. We're flying to the place where my grandfather and the other Sacred Beasts formed the cosmos, established the five seasons, and created the five elements."

"How can we possibly go that far?" asked Zhuzi.

"I fly faster than I walk!" the turtle said, laughing. "Climb on my back!"

After Zhuzi climbed on, the turtle commanded, "Hang on tight!"

They rose into the sky and flew at an inconceivable speed. Zhuzi looked down to see a blur of farms, villages, rivers, forests, cities, and mountains. Finally, they descended to the ground.

"My friends—the dragon and phoenix—are coming soon! I can't wait to see them. I've missed them all those years in the temple."

Zhuzi heard wings flapping and looked up to see an enormous blue dragon.

"Long time no see," the turtle called out. "Azure Dragon, it's good to see you again! Ha! You always thought you could fly faster than me, but I got here first!"

As the two old friends laughed together, Zhuzi heard wings flapping again and looked up to see the phoenix with its brilliant red, green, and yellow feathers. The three friends spent the day feasting, laughing, and catching up on everything they had been doing for the past few centuries.

Finally, as the sun slid toward the horizon, the turtle sighed. "I must fly back now. Zhuzi needs to get home before his father is worried sick."

"Here is one of my scales to remember me," the dragon said. When it touched Zhuzi's hand, it turned to gold.

"Here is a memento from me," said the phoenix, placing a fiery red plume in his hand.

Zhuzi climbed back on the turtle's back, and they flew through the drifting clouds. When they were nearly home, Zhuzi started dozing off and let go of the turtle's shell. He awakened to find himself slipping off the shell. Screaming, he plummeted toward the ground.

"Zhuzi! Zhuzi! Wake up!"

Zhuzi opened his eyes, certain he was dead. Looking around, he realized he was back in the temple, under the turtle! He looked up. The pillar was not broken! It was back on top of the turtle.

"You're covered in dust! Get out from under that turtle!"

Zhuzi was confused. "Am I dead?"

His father laughed. "You look alive to me! Have you been sleeping here all afternoon? Go wash yourself off. Your mother has dinner ready. I'm going to lock this temple now before any other miscreants try to sneak in."

Zhuzi rubbed his eyes and brushed off the dust, quietly asking himself, "Did everything really happen? Or was it all a dream?"

Roundup Activity: Thought Questions

1. How does the Pangu creation myth contrast with other creation stories that you know?

2. How does Pangu's myth explain things in nature and moral values?

3. The world remained incomplete until Pangu's death. What does this tell us about life and death in Chinese philosophy?

4. Yin and Yang were in chaos until they achieved harmony, leading to Pangu forming inside the egg. What Chinese values did this reflect?

5. Pangu struggled alone to push the sky up above Earth for eighteen thousand years. What values did he model?

6. What does the meaning of Shangdi's name tell us about who he was?

7. If you could use an oracle bone to find out something about the future, what would you ask?

8. If you had to rewrite a sacred book (like the Bible or Qur'an) from memory because the government burned all the copies, how much would you be able to write?

9. Which of the Four Sacred Beasts captures your imagination and why?

10. What are three things that the story of Bamboo and the Turtle suggests about the relationship between Zhuzi and his father?

Chapter 2: The Descent of the Goddess: Nuwa's Gift to Humanity

The myths of Nuwa and her brother Fuxi show themes of ingenuity, resilience, and selflessness. They explore the intersection between divine intervention and human progress. Nuwa's story is a powerful story of innovation overcoming challenges. She resonates with all of us as we discover our potential to create change and confront problems in life.

Huaxu, Primordial Ancestress Mother

Who created people in Chinese mythology? According to Taoist theology, Pangu's granddaughter created the first animals and people. But how could Pangu have a granddaughter if he died before having children? After he died, a primeval female named **Huaxu** emerged from his body. She was not exactly a goddess, at least. Taoists never worshiped her. She was also not human. She looked human from the waist up, but her lower body was a snake. Huaxu was the world's primordial ancestress in Taoist theology.

Gods and important people in Chinese mythology were often conceived in extraordinary ways. Huaxu's offspring were no exception. She got pregnant after stepping into the footprint of **Lei Gong**, the thunder god. This raises two questions. First, if her bottom half were a serpent, how could she step into anything? Did snakes have legs then?

Second, how did Lei Gong suddenly appear in the picture? The chronology was off for him to show up at the dawn of time. Why? Humans did not exist yet, and Lei Gong was originally human.

According to Chinese mythology, Lei Gong was a man who ate a peach from Heaven's peach tree orchard, which transformed him into a god. Myths often come from various sources, which makes them jumbled. The Chinese probably had an early folktale about Lei Gong and included him in the Taoist creation myth, which wasn't written until the 3rd century CE, after Taoism morphed from a philosophy into a religion. At any rate, after he became a god, Lei Gong had bat wings, a bird's beak, blue skin, and claws. Like the Norse god Thor, Lei Gong carried a hammer for making thunder.

The **Jade Emperor** (the Taoist chief god) told Lei Gong to kill evil people and demons but not to harm anyone else. However, wherever Lei Gong went, a dark cloud surrounded him, obscuring his sight. Sometimes, he killed the wrong person. One day, he accidentally killed a young woman named **Dianmu**, who was a rice farmer. When the Jade Emperor heard this, he was furious.

"Dianmu did not deserve to die, so I made her a goddess. Now, you must marry her and take care of her since you killed her."

Dianmu was the best thing to happen to Lei Gong. She accompanied him on his mission to execute evil people, using her mirrors to shine light on Earth. Lei Gong could see his target and not accidentally kill innocent people.

All of this happened long after Huaxu conceived twins from stepping in Lei Gong's footprint. Huaxu's son and daughter looked like her, with bodies that were half serpent and half human. They did not have Lei Gong's bat wings, blue skin, or claws. She named the boy **Fuxi** and the girl **Nuwa**. Then, Huaxu faded out of the picture, except that she was reportedly the ancestor of Huangdi, the Yellow Emperor.

Gonggong Breaks the Sky

By the time Fuxi and Nuwa were born, other gods were in the picture. One was **Gonggong**, the water god. Like Nuwa and her children, he was human-looking from the waist up but a serpent from the waist down. His head was copper, his forehead was iron, and he had red hair. Gonggong had a fiery temper and created mayhem wherever he went.

Another deity was **Zhurong**, the fire god. The Chinese characters in his name suggest a connection with worms, insects, and snakes. **Sima Qin**, a historian in the 1st century BCE, considered Zhurong a human, not a god. He was thought to be the brother of Gun, whose son Yu saved China from the **Great Flood**. Chinese mythology has two versions of the Great Flood. The first, covered in this chapter, was at the beginning of the world. The other, covered in Chapter 7, was a localized flooding of the Yellow and Yangtze Rivers that devastated China's ancient civilization for years.

For a fire god, Zhurong was not very fiery. He was inactive and apathetic while riding around on his flaming dragon. Yet, something finally stirred him out of his laziness. As a water god, Gonggong wanted to cover Earth with water. Zhurong intervened, and a celestial battle ensued. As lightning flashed and thunder rolled, Gonggong and Zhurong wrestled in the sky. The two gods fought night and day, but neither could prevail.

"Fight me on Earth!" Gonggong challenged Zhurong. Gonggong put his elite soldiers on a bamboo raft in the sea. But Zhurong was the fire god, and he shot a pillar of fire at the raft. The fire consumed the bamboo, sinking the raft and drowning the soldiers.

Gonggong was the water god, so he called up monsters from the sea that had bat wings, long horns, and impenetrable armor. Gonggong flung the monsters toward Zhurong in an immense wall of water. Zhurong shot out fire from his mouth, consuming Gonggong's monsters.

Realizing he was undone, Gonggong fled west as the other gods jeered. Blinded by rage, he crashed into **Mount Buzhou**, one of the **four pillars** holding up the sky. Gonggong fell backward, rubbing the knot on his head. Then, he felt a drop of water hit his face. Was it raining? A stream of water followed the drop, and then a gushing torrent. Gonggong had broken the sky. The floodwaters washed him away, never to be seen again.

Nuwa Repairs the Sky

Zhurong and the other gods looked on helplessly as the flood covered Earth. Mountains exploded, and earthquakes rumbled. Nuwa appeared on the scene, upset at Gonggong's carelessness and the other gods' inability to act.

"Blockheads! You are useless!" she scolded.

Nuwa scanned the area. How could she fix the sky?

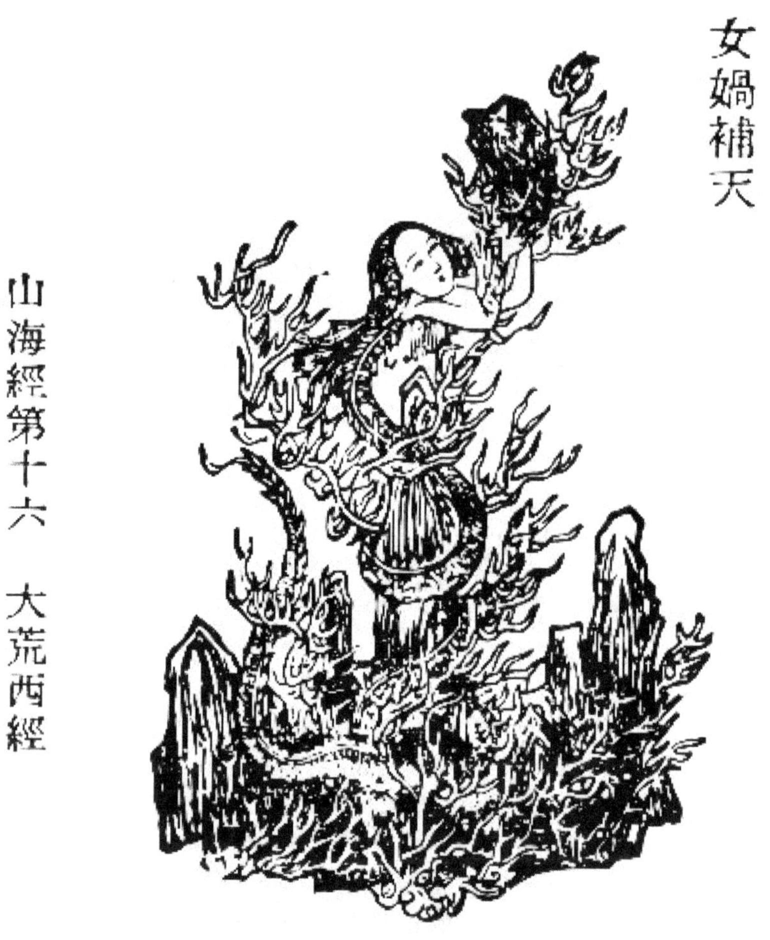

Nuwa stops the flood. [5]

Nuwa took five colored stones, melted them into one piece, and plugged the hole in the sky. The floodwaters receded. However, she also needed to mend Mount Buzhou, or the sky would fall again. As she looked around, she saw a huge black turtle lumbering along. Nuwa cut off its four legs and used them to prop up the sky. Despite her best efforts, Earth tilted in one direction and the sky in the other. That is why China's rivers flow from the west and empty into the eastern sea. However, the sun, moon, and stars move across the sky from east to west.

A Moral Dilemma

Nuwa sighed in relief as her twin brother, Fuxi, praised her. "You did it, Nuwa! You are amazing!"

The siblings slithered off together. But then, Fuxi frowned. "Everything on Earth has died. We're the only ones left. You should marry me."

Nuwa stopped slithering and turned toward her brother, scowling. "Fuxi! We cannot marry. You're my twin brother!"

"Heaven will let us!" Fuxi replied. "We need to repopulate Earth. Let's put it to the test. Climb to the top of this mountain and light a fire. I'll slither over to that mountain and light a fire at its top. If the smoke from our fires rises directly to Heaven, that means we should not marry. But if the smoke from each of our fires moves toward the other and joins in the middle, that is a sign that Heaven is blessing our marriage."

So, the brother and sister tested it out. The smoke from their two fires did travel toward the other. The plumes joined and swirled up to Heaven, so the siblings became husband and wife.

A painting of Nuwa and Fuxi from the Tang dynasty (618–907 CE)[6]

Nuwa Creates Animals and People

Now, it was time to repopulate Earth. Nuwa did the work, starting with the animals. On the first day, she made chickens. She created dogs on the second day and sheep on the third. On the fourth day, she made pigs, cows on the fifth, and horses on the sixth day. On the seventh day, she created humans. Nuwa gathered globs of yellow clay from the river and formed them into the shape of people. They had faces and upper bodies like hers and Fuzi's. But instead of a snake's lower body, her people had legs, feet, and toes. Using her divine power, Nuwa brought her clay figurines to life.

However, making the clay people was tiresome. Mending the sky had already exhausted Nuwa. She realized she had to create many humans to oversee Earth. Instead of individually shaping each clay human, she dragged a vine through the river mud, then swung it in circles over her head, flinging off the mud blobs. The blobs became ordinary people, while the yellow clay people that she shaped were the nobility. Nuwa made her people male and female, so they could have children.

Fuxi's Fishers and Farmers

Worn out from all her work, Nuwa died, but Fuxi lived for another two centuries. It was Fuxi's job to ensure that Nuwa's people could live. Fuxi taught them how to catch fish with their hands, so they would always have food to eat. However, this created trouble with the **Dragon King**, who ruled the rivers and sea. He complained, "The humans are eating all my fish! Soon, the fish will be gone, and I will have no one to rule!"

The tortoise, the Dragon King's prime minister, informed Fuxi, "The Dragon King decrees your people can no longer catch fish with their hands."

Fuxi frowned. How would his people eat? He pondered the question for a few days until a solution came to mind. During **_xiuxi_**, the **midday rest time**, Fuxi lay in the shade of a tree. He watched a spider weave a web and then quietly wait. Before long, a fly flew into the web, and the spider hurried over and wrapped it in silk. Fuxi used the idea of the web to weave a net from the riverside reeds. He practiced throwing it into the river to catch fish. Then, he called the humans over and showed them how to net fish.

By this time, people knew how to hunt animals, but the deer and mountain goats learned to run away when they saw humans.

"I know how to solve the problem!" Fuxi announced. "Instead of hunting, tame some animals. You can keep herds of sheep and cattle. Not only will you have meat, but you can also use their milk. Don't forget the birds. You can tame ducks and chickens for their eggs and meat."

Fuxi taught humans how to settle down, build houses, and be civilized. He introduced other ideas too, like marriage, money, and writing.

Huangdi, the "First Emperor"

Huangdi, the Yellow Emperor [7]

After Nuwa and Fuxi died, the humans divided into tribes, and wars began. Huangdi (whose name means "Yellow Emperor") was the first emperor. The Chinese had a habit of worshiping important leaders after they died, so the first emperor also became a god.

Huangdi may have been a real person. He supposedly ruled part of north-central China from 2679 to 2597 BCE. However, he did not accomplish everything that Chinese mythology claims he did. The Chinese did not begin writing until around 1600 BCE, and Huangdi, if he were a real person, lived a thousand years earlier. His stories would have been passed down orally for a millennium and likely embellished.

Huangdi's given name was Xuan Yuan. As previously mentioned, important people in Chinese mythology usually have something miraculous happen at their conception or birth. In Huangdi's case, a loud crack of thunder sounded when he was conceived, despite it being a cloudless day. Some of Huangdi's myths merged with Fuxi's, as they both taught people how to build houses and domesticate animals. However, legend says Huangdi even tamed bears and tigers. Both Fuxi and Huangdi supposedly taught people how to write; however, there is no evidence that the Chinese were writing until the Shang dynasty.

Ancient myths say that Huangdi introduced clothing to the Chinese people, but archaeological evidence shows that the Chinese wore clothing in the Neolithic era and even wove linen on looms. Huangdi also reportedly taught his people to sail in boats and use wheeled carts and chariots. He might have taught them to sail, but boats were already traveling in the Persian Gulf about three thousand years earlier. The archaeological record shows wheel tracks in Henan Province dating to around 2200 BCE, about four hundred years after Huangdi's supposed reign. However, the horse was not introduced to China until the Shang dynasty.

Legend says that Huangdi lived to the age of one hundred, perhaps due to using **Chinese traditional medicine**, which tradition says he introduced. He also supposedly developed the Chinese calendar, Chinese astronomy, higher math, and the first law code in China. Huangdi introduced the **cuju** ball game, in which players have to keep a ball in the air using only their feet, knees, heads, or shoulders. They cannot use their hands or let the ball touch the ground as they try to score a goal by sending the ball through a hoop.

Huangdi was the ruler of the Bear tribe. After defeating the neighboring Bull tribe, he merged the two groups. This caught the attention of a nearby supernatural tribe of eighty-one brothers, each of whom had eight arms and four eyes. Their leader, Chiyou, challenged Huangdi, who convinced eight neighboring tribes to help him. A horrific battle raged for days. Although Chiyou and his brothers had superpowers, Huangdi had more warriors. At first, he was winning.

But then, Chiyou blew a thick fog from his nose. Huangdi's army could see nothing, and they panicked. They tried to retreat but could not find their way off the battlefield. That was when Huangdi invented the "south-pointing" chariot. Its mechanisms always pointed south, allowing his men to get their bearings and start marching in the right direction. To stop them, Chiyou used his sorcery to whip up a typhoon. But Huangdi cried out to Heaven, and the gods turned the storm away.

Huangdi defeated Chiyou and his devilish brothers and became emperor of northern China. Many Chinese believed that Huangdi, the Yellow Emperor, became an immortal (or a god) when he died. He is still worshiped today as China's ancestral king.

Empress Leizu Invents Silk

Huangdi's wife, Leizu, reportedly introduced **silk** to China. However, archaeological evidence shows the Chinese were weaving silk centuries earlier. Her story claims she was sitting in her garden under a mulberry tree on a sweltering summer day. Suddenly, a silkworm cocoon fell from the tree into the cup of hot tea she was drinking. Leizu watched the cocoon dissolve and pulled on it with her finger. Stunningly, it was all one thread—over one thousand feet long!

The empress told Huangdi about her discovery. "The thread glistens and is so soft. I think I might weave it into the world's most luxurious fabric."

"Yes!" Huangdi nodded enthusiastically. "This is an astounding discovery. Study the matter carefully, and I'll send you all the help you need."

So, the empress spent weeks wandering among the mulberry trees in her garden. She learned that the silkworm moth laid eggs on mulberry leaves and that the larvae ate them after hatching. After about three weeks, the silkworms wove a cocoon around themselves. Leizu had her workers gather the silkworm cocoons and immerse them in boiling water to unravel the silk thread. She invented a reel to wind the thread around and a loom on which to weave the thread. China's silk production had begun!

Ladies pounding silk fabric to soften it[8]

Silk became a luxury clothing for Chinese aristocrats and also a valuable trade good. For approximately two thousand years, silk weaving was a closely guarded state secret, granting China a monopoly on the lucrative silk trade.

Roundup Activity: Thought Questions

1. How did Lei Gong's punishment for accidentally killing Dianmu turn out to be a blessing?

2. What do you think stirred Zhurong out of his apathy to fight Gonggong?

3. Gonggong's blinding rage after his defeat caused him to crash into Mount Buzhou. What lesson can we learn about the dangers of unchecked ego?

4. Who (besides Gonggong) made Nuwa angry after Gonggong broke the sky? Why?

5. Imagine you are Nuwa, fixing the sky. What materials would you use in today's world to repair the Heavens?

6. Nuwa created humans from yellow clay. If you had the power to create a new creature, what would it be like and why?

7. Fuxi is known for his helpfulness and compassion toward humans. Can you think of a time when someone showed you unexpected kindness or help? How did it make you feel?

8. What do you think would surprise Nuwa the most if she visited the modern world?

9. Based on Huangdi's myths, what do you think were the three qualities of an ideal leader for the Chinese?

10. Chinese myth credits a female with creating humans and another woman with developing silk manufacturing. What do you think this says about the innovative or creative role of women in Chinese culture?

Chapter 3: Journey to Immortality: The Quest of the Eight Immortals

This chapter delves into the adventures of the **Eight Immortals**, each of whom embodies distinct virtues and passes through unique trials to achieve immortality. Their stories illustrate perseverance, diversity, and moral excellence. Myths of the Eight Immortals also offer valuable insights into overcoming obstacles and achieving one's goals, even when it means taking a different path.

The Religion Behind the Myths

Before diving into the story of the Eight Immortals, we should first lay the groundwork of Chinese philosophy and religion. Knowing the basics helps in understanding the myths. Since China did not have writing before the Shang dynasty (1600–1046 BCE), we must rely on archaeological evidence to understand what religion might have been like before then. Artifacts suggest that the early Chinese worshiped their ancestors, things in nature, and possibly dragons. The vast ritual complexes at the **Erlitou archaeological site**, believed to have been a capital of the Xia dynasty (2070–1600 BCE), point to a **centralized state religion.**

As previously mentioned, by the Shang dynasty, the Chinese were worshiping Shangdi as their supreme god. They believed he had existed from the beginning of time and had created Heaven, Earth, people, and all other life. Shangdi was probably worshiped during the Xia dynasty or perhaps earlier. However, the Chinese did not create idols or artwork featuring Shangdi's image. Without written evidence, it is difficult to know when his worship began.

Besides worshiping Shangdi, the Shang dynasty Chinese also offered animal sacrifices to their **ancestors** and to guardians of nature, such as the sun and moon. The Zhou dynasty (1046–256 BCE) that followed continued worshiping Shangdi, their ancestors, and nature spirits. However, they used the word **"Tian "** interchangeably with Shangdi and gradually shifted to using Tian almost exclusively. Tian could mean either Heaven or the highest god.

The Zhou dynasty experienced a period of political instability when power shifted to its new capital, Changzhou, in the east. Despite the chaos, China had a cultural surge in the **Spring and Autumn Period** (772–476 BCE), a time when poets, musicians, and philosophers left an unforgettable mark on Chinese history.

A Western Han (202 BCE–9 CE) fresco of Confucius by an unknown Chinese painter [9]

Master K'ung (Confucius), Laozi (Lao Tzu), and Mozi were the main philosophers of the era called the **Hundred Schools of Thought. Confucius** emphasized social harmony and how political leaders should model morality, loyalty, and respect. He encouraged everyone to grow in knowledge and good behavior. He said people should show respect, obedience, and love to their parents and ancestors.

Mozi taught that a person should love everyone, including strangers, and strive to do what is best for all, rather than prioritizing one's own interests. He believed that society should value labor and increase productivity by utilizing efficient methods. Instead of war, he encouraged people to do everything possible to live together in peace and to use diplomacy to resolve conflicts.

Laozi taught the philosophy of **Taoism** (Daoism), which eventually developed into a religion. He believed that "**Tao**" (or "**Dao**") was not a god but an indescribable, unnamable, abstract concept. It always existed, was the source of everything, and was the process that governed the universe. Language could not describe Tao; a person had to experience it intuitively. Tao was the natural order and the universe's rhythm.

If a person wanted to become "one" with Tao, they had to stay uninvolved with the world. They should be humble, live simply, and release their attachments to anyone and anything. Instead of trying to make things happen or change things, they should empty their minds and just let nature take its course.

While philosophies were springing up in China, Siddhartha Gautama (the **Buddha**) was introducing a new teaching in India. Born into a royal family around 563 BCE, he desired to end suffering and seek enlightenment. He left his family and, at age thirty-five, achieved **nirvana** (enlightenment). For the rest of his life, he traveled around teaching his disciples. **Buddhism** arrived in China during the Han dynasty (206 BCE–220 CE). We will focus more on Buddhism and its teachings in Chapter 7.

Buddhism's arrival in China stirred discontent among Taoists. Buddhists built monasteries where followers could meditate and learn the Buddhist scriptures. Taoism had no organized scriptures and no monasteries at that time. Taoism was a vague philosophy that most people found hard to understand, with no gods to worship.

Because of this, Taoist leaders transformed Taoism from a philosophy into a religion, complete with scriptures, monasteries, monks, and deities. **Zhang Daoling**, a Taoist teacher, founded the Celestial Masters school and made Taoism the state religion of Sichuan Province. The new pantheon of Taoist gods features in several myths in this book, including the **Eight Immortals**. We will unpack more about the Taoist chief god, the **Jade Emperor**, and his family in Chapter 5.

What Is an Immortal?

In ancient China, particularly in Buddhism and Taoism, a **Xian**, or immortal, was a human who had achieved eternal life or immortality. A man or woman—even a teen—could do this through various means. One was **alchemy**, where a person would eat or drink certain substances, such as mercury, mother-of-pearl, or gold, to break the power of death. They often killed themselves by eating dangerous substances while trying to live forever.

Another way was extreme fasting. Buddhist sages typically ate only one meal: breakfast. If they were seeking immortality, it would be a minimal breakfast. Many Taoist sages avoided grains and meat, eating only vegetables. Other people tried to achieve immortality by holding their breath, meditating, or using other methods described in the Taoist book *Tao Te Ching.*

The few who reached immortal status had not only conquered death but could reportedly do supernatural things. For example, they could fly, do magic, and shapeshift into mountain hermits, mystical creatures, or divine beings. In Buddhism, not all immortals lived forever. Some lived exceptionally long lives but eventually died. In Taoism, immortality meant that both the body and soul lived forever. Taoists believed that when their **qi** (vital energy) stopped flowing, they would die. They used techniques they believed enhanced qi, such as maintaining a peaceful life in tune with nature.

Statue of Jiang Ziya at Weihe Park in Zhucheng, China[10]

Jiang Ziya, the Man Who Abandoned Immortality for a Different Destiny

Jiang Ziya was a military general and the first king of the Qi state, part of the Zhou dynasty. His impoverished family abandoned him at birth, but a wealthy woman found him in the wild and adopted him. Even as a child, Ziya's goal was to become immortal. Taoism and Buddhism were not yet established in China in Ziya's time. The Chinese of his era believed that one could achieve eternal life through heroic deeds, divine gifts, or by living on a mountain and meditating.

As an older teenager, Jiang Ziya set off to find a master who would teach him the secrets of immortality. Instead, he met a divine creature, who gave him a message from Heaven. "Your future is not with the immortals. Heaven has a different assignment for you. The Shang dynasty has lost the Mandate of Heaven for their cruelty, corruption, immorality, and excessive drinking. Your destiny is to end the Shang dynasty!"

Emperor Zhou was the ruler of the Shang dynasty. He was obsessed with his concubine Daji, who was actually a **fox spirit**—a nine-tailed creature that could shapeshift into a woman and was usually devious. Daji encouraged Emperor Zhou (not to be confused with the Zhou dynasty that replaced him) to commit evil deeds, such as torturing his officials. His people endured crushing taxes to support his lavish and decadent lifestyle.

At first, Jiang Ziya served in Emperor Zhou's court, but the monarch was so insufferable that Jiang Ziya left to be a hermit. That was when King Wen of Zhou found him.

The province of Zhou was part of the Shang dynasty, so King Wen was a vassal king, subordinate to Emperor Zhou. King Wen was going hunting one day and asked his fortune-tellers if he would be successful.

They told him, "Yes, you will be successful on the north bank of the Wei River. You will not catch a tiger or any other beast. Instead, you will find a nobleman sent by Heaven to teach you. If you make him your advisor, you and your descendants will thrive."

King Wen did not eat meat for the next three days, purifying himself to meet the Heaven-sent teacher. The king found Jiang Ziya at the river, sitting on a grass mat and fishing. Oddly, his hook was a straight piece of metal. How could it catch a fish? Nevertheless, the king courteously greeted Jiang Ziya. After talking with him, King Wen discovered that Jiang Ziya had a razor-sharp grasp of politics and warfare. He took Jiang Ziya back with him to be his prime minister.

After the king died, Jiang Ziya continued to serve his son, King Wu. The young king immediately wanted to lead an insurrection against the Shang emperor, Zhou. Yet, Jiang Ziya advised him to wait. "The type is not ripe yet. We must be patient."

Eventually, Jiang Ziya felt everything was in place to overturn the oppressive ruler. He led King Wu's troops into the mighty **Battle of Muye** as the drums pounded. With only one hundred men, he drew Emperor Zhou's soldiers away, allowing the rest of the army to surround and conquer the city. King Wu took control, and the Zhou dynasty ruled China for eight centuries.

King Wu made Jiang Ziya the duke of Qi (Shandong province today) and "Master of Strategy" over his government. Jiang Ziya advised King Wu that China would only remain strong if the ordinary people prospered. Although Taoism had not yet emerged, Taoists later worshiped Jiang Ziya as a war god.

Who Were the *Ba Qian* (Eight Immortals)?

These immortals were part of Taoist mythology. Most of them were likely real people who lived during the Tang dynasty (618–907 CE) or the Song dynasty (960–1279 CE). Through religious devotion, deception, or sheer luck, they achieved immortal status. Chinese art usually shows them together as a group rather than as individuals. The Eight Immortals defied traditional religious norms by disregarding gender, age, and social status within their group.

Immortals were typically perceived as hermits living on a mountain who ate little and rode around on dragons. The Eight Immortals broke the mold, as they spent time together (usually floating around in a boat), getting drunk, singing, and playing guessing games. Despite their spiritual status, they all had flaws. They liked drinking so much that legend says they introduced "Drunken Kung Fu" to China. As a group, they fought corruption, cruelty, and wickedness. They lived together on an island in the Yellow Sea (between China and Korea). No one disturbed them on their island because the water surrounding it was "weak" and could not support normal boats.

A mural of the Eight Immortals in a temple in Hue, Vietnam [11]

Li Tieguai (Iron-Crutch Li) (Li Xuan)

Artwork of this immortal typically depicts him as a stout, elderly man with a disheveled appearance. He often walks with an iron crutch. Of the eight, he was the first to receive immortality. The Jade Emperor's wife, Xi Wanmu, Queen Mother of the West, gave him the **Elixir of the Gods**, a potion that granted eternal life.

How did he become lame? Li Xuan had abandoned all his possessions to seek spiritual goals. He became adept at **astral travel**, an out-of-body experience where he traveled in his spirit to other realms. After one journey, he could not find his body when he returned, so he took up residence in the body of a crippled beggar who had just died. Li Xuan's crippled leg sometimes made him irritable, yet he was always kind to the poor and sick. He carried a magic gourd containing celestial medicine, which he used to heal people.

One day, Li Xuan wanted to cross a river but could not find a boat or a bridge. He picked up a large leaf, stepped on it, and floated across the river. A man nearby stared at this incredible act. "Climb aboard!" Li Xuan invited him.

"I don't know how you're staying afloat," the man answered. "Yet, I know that leaf will surely sink if I step on it with you."

"I'm afraid you're right," sighed Li Xuan. "Human thoughts are heavy. They weigh one down."

Zhongli Quan

Zhongli Quan lived as a mortal in the Han dynasty, where he served as a military general. One day, an enemy army defeated his forces, and he escaped into the mountains, where he met an ancient hermit. The old man taught him the secret rituals and substances to drink to become immortal.

Zhongli Quan is typically depicted as a heavyset elderly man, holding a white feather or fan, with an open gown revealing his potbelly. His fan could bring the dead back to life and change stones into silver or gold. He used his superpowers to help the needy and oppressed.

Eight immortals: He Xiangu stands in the stern holding the rudder. Clockwise from her are Han Xiang Zi, Lan Caihe, Li Tieguai, Lu Dongbin, Zhongli Quan, and Cao Guojiu. Zhang Guo Lao is riding his donkey over the sea.[12]

Lu Dongbin

As an older teenager, Lu Dongbin failed the imperial examination, which closed the door to a civil service career. Depressed and unsure what to do next, he wandered around until he came to an inn. Zhongli Quan was in the same inn, warming brandy. Lu Dongbin grew sleepy as he watched the older man. He dreamed he had passed the examinations and gone on to enjoy a successful political career for fifty years, becoming fabulously wealthy as the prime minister. However, everything suddenly went wrong when he was accused of wrongdoing. He lost all his wealth and was exiled.

Lu Dongbin awakened from his dream to see Zhongli Quan still warming his brandy. He realized that even if he had pursued his royal career, he might have ended up where he was at that point: wandering about with no job.

He decided to pursue immortality as a disciple of Zhongli Quan. To achieve immortality, he had to pass ten trials to prove his detachment from the world. For instance, he could not weep at the death of a loved one, and he had to lose all his possessions without caring. His most challenging test was overcoming temptation for a beautiful woman.

Pictures of Lu Dongbin show him holding a sword to fight evil spirits. Once he achieved immortality, he assisted others along the same path. He even helped trees become immortal. He helped a willow tree and a plum tree be reincarnated as a man and a woman, who married and opened a teahouse. Lu Dongbin then guided them on the path to immortality.

He Xiangu

He Xiangu was the only female in the group. Pictures of He Xiangu often show her wearing pink and holding a white lotus flower or wearing a collar that resembles one. When depicted with the seven male immortals, she is typically shown standing at the stern of a boat, holding the rudder.

When He Xiangu was twelve, she was picking tea on a mountain when she met Lu Dongbin. He was there to guide her in becoming immortal using alchemy. First, he told her to eat mica that was ground into powder. Mica is a sparkly mineral that comes in thin, flexible sheets. Powdered mica is used today in lip gloss and eye shadow to create a shimmering effect.

Lu Dongbu explained, "Eating mica will make you lightweight and delicate as you begin your path to becoming immortal. You should also eat only a small amount of food. Finally, stay away from the boys! No sexual relations."

He Xiangu did what Lu Dongbu told her, becoming extremely thin. When she was about fifteen, her parents arranged a marriage for her. Yet, she slipped away on the night of her wedding, leaving a note for her parents. "Marriage will distract me from the path the gods have set for me. I am leaving to ride the celestial crane to immortality."

He Xiangu rides the celestial crane[18]

He Xiangu began eating mother-of-pearl, which helped her to transcend the limits of her physical body. She could leave her body and fly to the mountains, where she collected herbs to use to heal people. The white lotus flower was her symbol because it represents harmony and health.

Lan Caihe

Lan Caihe was a man who sometimes wore women's clothing and carried a basket of flowers (or fruit) with medicinal properties that promoted longevity. Before becoming an immortal, he was a homeless street performer who traveled from town to town, singing "foot-stomping" philosophical songs for the coins people would toss.

Artwork of Lan Caihe shows him as a teen, often holding castanets, cymbals, or a clapper to keep rhythm while singing. He also sometimes played the flute. Legend said he did not age, even before becoming immortal, and that he was actually decades older than his adolescent appearance. He wore a shoe on only one foot; his bare foot was a symbol of immortality. Lan Caihe's path to becoming immortal was not through meditation or eating weird things but through goodness.

Despite being a beggar himself, Lan Caihe showed exceptional kindness to the poor. With the coins he earned from singing, he bought his own meals and drinks, then gave any remaining money to other needy people. One day, he saw an old man (Li Tieguai in disguise) with horrible sores on his feet. Lan Caihe put medicinal herbs on the old man's feet, healing the sores. Shortly after, he became immortal while sitting at a table outside a tavern, drinking. The white crane of immortality flew up and landed at his table, and Lan Caihe perched on its back and rode to Heaven.

Han Xiangzi

This immortal was a musical prodigy and poet, usually pictured holding a flute. When he was a child, both of his parents died. His uncle raised him. He sent Han Xiangzi to a Confucian school when he was a young teen to prepare for a career in political administration. Yet, Han Xiangzi was bored. His uncle thought he might be more suited to a religious career, so he sent him to a Buddhist school; however, Xiangzi was still bored.

One day, he was walking with his uncle, and he picked a flower. "Look, Daye!" He showed his uncle. "I changed the color of this peony!"

Xiangzi realized Heaven had gifted him with special abilities. Against his uncle's wishes, he began studying Taoism under the guidance of Lu Dongbin and Zhongli Quan. His uncle tried to distract him by arranging a marriage to a pretty young lady. Xiangzi liked her but would not sleep with her because he wanted to become immortal. He finally achieved his goal and then returned home to guide his uncle, aunt, and wife to immortality.

Cao Guojiu

"Uncle Cao" was the brother of the empress during the Song dynasty and an important official in the royal court. However, the palace was filled with corruption and greed. His brother, also an official, fell into dishonest ways. Cao Guojiu tried to reform his brother and paid his gambling debts. His brother barely escaped losing his head because of his crime, and many in the palace suspected that Cao Guojiu was equally guilty.

It was a wake-up call. Guojiu realized he needed to leave the corrupt court drama and pursue a different life. He gave all his money to people experiencing poverty and settled down to a peaceful life in the countryside, where he met Zhongli Quan and Lu Dongbin. He studied Taoism under them until he achieved immortality. Guojiu is usually pictured wearing a court official's robe and "futou" turban with wing-like projections on each side.

Zhang Guolao

The artwork of this immortal portrays him as an old man with a long white beard, often riding a donkey. Sometimes, he rides the donkey backward. In his mortal life, Zhang Guolao was an expert in alchemy and could supposedly speak with the dead. He did odd things, like drink dew from poisonous flowers and snatch birds out of the sky. His white donkey carried him for a thousand miles each day. He loved to make wine, which the rest of the immortals enjoyed drinking. As a martial arts master, he was so agile that he could bend backward until his shoulders touched the ground.

One day, Guolao suddenly dropped dead while he was worshiping in a temple. His body decomposed immediately, but several days later, he was walking around, alive and well. Many years later, after extensive Taoist studies, he died again while living as a hermit on Zhongtiao Mountain. His disciples buried him in a tomb, but when they returned to honor him a few days later, his body had disappeared.

Roundup Activity: Thought Questions

1. Why do you think the Chinese did not make idols or have artwork with Shangdi's image?

2. Which of the three philosophers (Confucius, Mozi, and Laozi) do you most agree with and why?

3. How does the ancient Chinese concept of immortality compare to your own beliefs?

4. If you were Jiang Ziya, would you give up the chance for immortality to solve the political problems in your country?

5. Each of the Eight Immortals has unique powers and attributes. Which immortal do you relate to the most, and why?

6. If you could go on an adventure with the Eight Immortals, what kind of challenge would you want to face together, and how would you contribute to overcoming it?

7. The Eight Immortals come from diverse backgrounds with different strengths. How do their stories teach us about teamwork and valuing a range of skills?

8. Imagine you could interview one of the Eight Immortals. Whom would you choose, and what would you ask them?

9. The Eight Immortals use their powers to help others and fight evil. How can we apply the moral lessons from their adventures to our daily lives, especially in helping our community?

10. What path to immortality would you rather take?

Chapter 4: The Emperor's Secret: The Elixir of Life

The ancient Chinese were obsessed with immortality. Myths have evolved around Emperor Qin, a historical ruler who wanted to live forever. He sent ships to search for the magical Penglai, home of the Eight Immortals. He then embarked on a relentless hunt for the Elixir of Life, which led him to the brink of madness and despair.

The **Legend of the White Snake** intertwines love, deception, and the pursuit of eternal life. It provides a captivating exploration of the lengths to which individuals might go to escape the clutches of death.

These stories explore the human desire to overcome mortality, the ethical dilemmas this desire creates, and the acceptance of life's natural rhythms. They encourage us to ponder the value of life, the consequences of our choices, and the importance of living meaningfully.

Emperor Qin and the Quest for Immortality

Emperor Qin Shi Huang established the short-lived Qin dynasty (221-206 BCE). He is often called the first emperor, although earlier dynasties with emperors preceded him, such as the Xia, Shang, and Zhou dynasties. The Qin dynasty is sometimes called China's first dynasty because it formed a unified state after the Warring States era splintered China. The Qin dynasty covered more territory than earlier dynasties and established a centralized administration under a single ruler.

Many people desire eternal life. For some, this means one's spirit continues to exist after the physical body dies. However, the Chinese immortals lived on in their physical bodies. That was what Emperor Qin wished for. Two assassination attempts made him realize he could suddenly lose his life. He needed to stay alive for the sake of a unified China.

These plots happened before he became emperor, when he was in his twenties and known as Ying Zheng. He was fighting to bring the warring states under one government, but the rulers of some states resisted his efforts. Crown Prince Dan of the state of Yan planned the first assassination attempt. He sent two teenage diplomats to Ying Zheng with a gruesome gift: the head of Fan Yuqi, one of Ying Zheng's generals who had defected to the enemy.

The assassins presented Ying Zheng with Fan Yuqi's head, and he nodded in approval.

"There's more, sire," the older teen, named Jing Ki, said, smiling. "This scroll is a map of Dukang. It will be helpful in your plans of attack for that region."

Ying Zheng raised an eyebrow and reached for the map. While he was studying it, he saw movement out of the corner of his eye. Jing Ki was lunging at him with a dagger! Ying Zheng threw himself to the side just in time, although the knife cut his sleeve. He tried to pull out his sword, but in his panic, he could not get it out of its sheath. So, he jumped up and ran behind a pillar, with Jing Ki chasing after him.

At that moment, the royal doctor walked in and saw Jing Ki chasing Ying Zheng around the pillar. He threw his medicine bag at the murderous teen, knocking him off balance. Ying Zheng finally got his sword out and killed Jing Ki, then collapsed on his throne. He stared into space for hours, shivering. For the rest of his days, he kept his sword lying on his lap.

Jing Ki had a friend named Gao Jianli, who decided to finish what Jing Ki was supposed to do. Gao Jianli was a well-known player of a stringed instrument called the zhu. One day, he approached Ying Zheng, offering to play his zhu. But one of Ying Zheng's attendants knew who he was.

"Sire! Don't let him near you! I know that boy. He's Jing Ki's friend." Ying Zheng had to kill him, which made him sad because he never got to hear him play the zhu.

Ying Zheng finally conquered the warring states and became Emperor Qin of a unified China. His desire for immortality continued. However, he could not spend years meditating or starving himself. After all, he was the emperor. He had a country to run. He needed to build the Great Wall of China, connecting and shoring up the preexisting sections. Emperor Qin needed a different path to immortality.

Search for Penglai

"Xu Fu!" the emperor spoke to his sorcerer. "How can I live forever?"

Xu Fu pulled on his beard and thought. "Well, sire, there is Penglai, the island home of the Eight Immortals. It has a high, snow-covered mountain named Fanghu, where the immortals live in a silver and gold palace. They say the fruit on the island is magic. It can cure sickness, make one forever young, and revive the dead."

"Where is it?" asked Emperor Qin.

"It's in the Bohai Sea, at the eastern end."

"Go there!" commanded the emperor. "Bring back the fruit from the island."

A woodcut of one of Xu Fu's ships [14]

"Well, sire, you need to send tribute. Boys and girls."

"Yes! Yes!" waved the emperor. "Take five hundred of the most beautiful children you can find. Take precious gifts in ten beautiful ships for the Eight Immortals."

So, Xu Fu set sail with ten exquisite ships and five hundred lovely boys and girls. He sailed around the Bohai Sea, but he could not find the mythical island. He sailed back home, and Emperor Qin asked him if he had found the island.

"No, sire. A giant sea creature blocked my path. I need to go back with archers to kill the monster."

Xu Fu sailed back to the Bohai Sea but never returned. Legend said he found a land of his own and became its king with the five hundred beautiful children.

The Elixir of Life

When Emperor Qin realized Xu Fu was not coming back, he fell into a depression, feeling hopeless. But then he perked up. "If Xu Fu isn't bringing back the magical fruit, there must be another way to achieve immortality. I must find the Elixir of Life!"

Wooden slats with writing on them were found at the bottom of a well in Hunan Province in 2002. The inscriptions recorded Emperor Qin's executive order to find the Elixir of Life (a liquid concoction that would keep someone alive forever) and awkward responses from his governors. One governor suggested that a certain herb growing on a sacred mountain might help the emperor live forever.

Emperor Qin called his **alchemists**, people who used a combination of chemistry, medicine, metallurgy, and mysticism to cure disease and prolong life. "Find me the magic potion! I must have the Elixir of Life!"

The potions the alchemists gave him contained **cinnabar**, a red mercury sulfide. This was dangerous; it could cause mercury poisoning, damaging the kidneys and brain. They may also have given him potions containing powdered gold or *Ganoderma* mushrooms. Chinese traditional medicine still uses this mushroom today to treat inflammation, cancer, neurodegenerative diseases, and cardiovascular problems. However, too much can cause liver toxicity and other serious issues.

What About the Afterlife?

Emperor Qin drank the elixirs his alchemists gave him, but he was still uneasy. Who knew if they were working? What if he died? Would he live forever in the next life? He called his scholars and asked them about the afterlife. No one had a straightforward answer.

"Master K'ung said we cannot know anything about life after death," said the Confucian scholars.

"Your spirit will be reabsorbed into Tao," said the Taoist scholars.

Emperor Qin frowned. "None of that makes sense! Why have we always worshiped our ancestors? Our spirits must continue to live after our bodies die."

The emperor began preparing for life after death in case the elixirs failed. He had his tomb built, and in nearby pits, he had clay figurines of over eight thousand soldiers, horses, and chariots buried. The **terracotta warriors** would serve him in the afterlife.

Qin Shi Huang's army of terracotta warriors [15]

Stinky Fish

Emperor Qin died when he was only forty-nine. His death was a mystery. He had been on a tour, traveling around the country, and died in Xingtai, Hebei Province, almost five hundred miles away from his capital of Xianyang (near today's Xi'an). How did he die? One theory is that the mercury in the Elixir of Life killed him.

When they discovered him dead, Emperor Qin's chief eunuch, Zhao Gao, and his prime minister, Li Si, conspired to hide the emperor's death. They wanted to get back to Xianyang before anyone knew so they could manipulate who the next emperor would be. However, it would take weeks to travel back, and the emperor's body would decompose. They arranged for wagons of *chou yu* (stinky fish, a salted fermented fish) to go in front and behind the emperor's chariot to cover up the stench of his body.

The Legend of the White Snake

Snakes are a symbol of immortality and transformation in Chinese culture because they shed their skins, representing the cycle of new birth. Some Chinese believe that the shedding of skin represents peeling off feelings of stress, unease, and bitterness that weigh a person down. When a person releases these negative thoughts, it frees them to enjoy healing and renewed life.

The Legend of the White Snake relates to immortality on several levels. First, Bai Suzhen, the central character, transformed from a snake spirit into a woman and then embarked on a quest for immortality. When her mortal husband died, she brought him back to life. After many struggles, sacrifices, and spiritual cultivation, Bai Suchen's friend, Xiao Mei, reached immortality. However, in some versions of the story, Bai Suchen gave up immortality to enjoy happiness on Earth. Although immortality is a central theme, the Legend of the White Snake is an endearing love story celebrating the affection between best friends, husband and wife, and parents and their child.

Bai Suzhen's life started as a snake spirit, which could be good or evil in Chinese mythology. She was a wicked demon. One day, a man named Xu Xian saved her from death. Yes, Chinese demons *could* die—they had physical, flesh-and-blood bodies. Xu Xian's intervention created a shift in her nature. Bai Suzhen no longer aspired to be a villain. Instead, she wanted to become a real woman and repay Xu Xian's kindness by being compassionate toward others.

Her transformation from a snake spirit into a female human took a long time. She had to spend a thousand years meditating on Mount Emei. Finally, Suzhen became a mortal woman. Her next goal was to become immortal. She studied under the Taoist goddess Lishan Laomu on Mount Li and tried to be good to all people and animals.

One day, she was walking down a mountain path when she saw a beggar capture a little green snake. He planned to sell its gall to a doctor of Chinese traditional medicine, which has used snake gall for millennia to treat arthritis, eye problems, and skin diseases. Bai Suzhen offered to buy the snake to save it from death, and the beggar agreed. Then she realized that the snake, named Xiao Qing (Little Green), was a snake spirit, as she had been.

Bai Suzhen and Xiao Qing became inseparable friends, and the little green snake spirit decided she also wanted to become a woman. She achieved her goal after studying Taoism for seven hundred years and promised Bai Suzhen she would never leave her. Bai Suzhen smiled and called her Xiao Mei (Little Sister).

One spring afternoon, everyone was celebrating **Tomb Sweeping Day**, cleaning the ancient graves and leaving flowers, food, and drink for their ancestors. Bai Suzhen and Xiao Mei were at West Lake in Hangzhou and crossed the Broken Bridge. The picturesque stone arch bridge was not actually broken. In the winter, the sun melted the snow on the southern side, but the northern side's snow cover made it appear as if it were not there.

As the ladies crossed the bridge, a spring shower fell. Suddenly, someone held an umbrella over their heads. Bai Suzhen turned to see a handsome young man. She smiled at his manners. Then, she looked at him closely. Where had she seen him before? Ah! Now she remembered. He was Xu Xian! In a past life, he was the man who had saved her from death when she was a white snake spirit. Now, they were both human!

She smiled at him, and he smiled back. They fell in love, got married, and opened a medicine shop, using the training Bai Suzhen had gained in her studies to be immortal (a goal she had not yet achieved). Soon, Bai Suzhen became pregnant, and they joyfully looked forward to the birth of their baby.

Their happy family soon met trouble when Fahai, a Buddhist monk, recognized Bai Suzhen. He knew she had been a white snake spirit. Fahai warned Xu Xian of his wife's true identity, but he refused to believe it. So, the monk told Xu Xian to give Bai Suzhen realgar wine, which contained arsenic sulfide. The **Dragon Boat Festival** was approaching, a time when people drank the special wine while enjoying the boat races. They thought it got rid of sickness, bad luck, and insects. When Bai Suzhen drank the realgar wine, she turned into a huge white snake.

"Ai ya!" ("Oh no!") screamed Xu Xian and dropped dead of a heart attack.

"Sweetheart! Don't die! I cannot live without you!" screeched Bai Suzhen.

"Quick, Bai Suzhen! Use your medical arts!" urged Xiao Mei.

Bai Suzhen dashed to the Kunlun Mountains, where a special herb grew. She rushed back to her husband and revived him with the magical plant.

"Bai Suzhen! Thank you for saving me. But you are really scary! Now that I know you're a snake spirit, I'm afraid to be around you."

Xu Xian wandered away in a fog of fear and bewilderment. Fahai approached him and warned, "You must go live at the Jinshan Temple. That is the only way you can save yourself from the snake demons. You know, your wife is not the only snake spirit. Xiao Mei is one too! You are not safe with those two!"

Fahai lured Xu Xian to the temple, where he imprisoned him. Bai Suzhen tried to rescue her husband, but because she was pregnant, her powers were limited. She sadly returned to Xiao Mei at the Broken Bridge. Eventually, Xu Xian overcame his fear of his wife and, with the help of a young monk, escaped from the temple and raced home. He found Bai Suzhen and Xiao Mei at the bridge.

"Bai Suzhen! I love you! I'm sorry for having left. Please forgive me."

Xiao Mei lunged at him in anger. "How dare you! You abandoned your wife when she was pregnant!"

"Xiao Mei! Stop! I love him!" Bai Suzhen cried.

The couple reconciled, and soon, Bai Suzhen gave birth to a baby boy, whom they named Shilin ("Forest Scholar").

However, Fahai caught up with the couple and, using his superpowers, imprisoned Bai Suzhen under the Leifeng Pagoda. Xu Xian had no idea where his wife was and wandered around China, searching for her. Finally, Xu Xian discovered his wife was under the Leifeng Pagoda, but he could not break Fahai's sorcery. Deeply grieved, he became a monk and lived at a monastery near the pagoda.

Meanwhile, Xiao Mei cared for baby Shilin while vowing to avenge her friend. She took the baby with her to Mount Emei so she could study, meditate, and gain more supernatural strength. As Shilin grew up, he would travel to the Leifeng Pagoda to light incense for his mother, vowing he would rescue her one day.

After twelve years, Xiao Mei had learned special arts that she used to attack Fahai, who dashed off and hid inside a giant crab shell. The Leifeng Pagoda fell over, setting Bai Suzhen free. Xu Xian left the monastery, and the happy family reunited. Xiao Mei continued to meditate until she finally achieved immortality and became a goddess.

Roundup Activity: Thought Questions

1. Why do you think Emperor Qin wanted to live forever?

2. Do you think immortality would be a blessing or a curse?

3. Imagine you're the first emperor and you've just discovered immortality isn't real. How would you feel? What would you do next?

4. Emperor Qin had the terracotta warriors built to accompany him in the afterlife. Do you believe in life after death? If so, how are you preparing for it?

5. Do you think Emperor Qin's fear of death ironically contributed to it? Have you ever done something hoping to make things better, only to make matters worse?

6. The Legend of the White Snake is about love and immortality. What would you do for the sake of love?

7. Would you rather experience joy in this life—with happy friendships, marriage, and children—or live forever?

8. In what ways was Xiao Mei a faithful friend to Bai Suzhen?

9. If you were married and your spouse suddenly morphed into a snake, what would you do?

10. The monk Fahai, thinking he was doing the right thing, separated a family. Have you ever thought you were doing (or saying) the right thing but ended up hurting someone?

Chapter 5: The Weaver and the Cowherd: A Love Story Written in the Stars

This chapter covers three celebrated love stories from Chinese mythology. The first myth is the touching tale of forbidden love between the **Weaver Girl and the Cowherd**, which led to their separation by the Milky Way. The story of **Chang'e** parallels this narrative of enduring love and separation. She sacrificed her earthly life, leaving her beloved husband behind, which explores the theme of love transcending physical boundaries. The **Butterfly Lovers**, whose story still plays regularly on Chinese television, features teenage lovers separated by circumstances beyond their control.

This chapter also talks about the Jade Emperor and his wife, whose decisions impact the lovers in the first two stories.

How the Jade Emperor Became the Supreme God

Zhang Daoling, proclaiming himself the first Celestial Master, transformed Taoism from a philosophy into a religion with a pantheon of deities during the Eastern Han dynasty (25–220 CE). He treated Laozi, the founder of Taoism, as a divine figure known as the "Most High Lord Lao." Zhang did not invent an entirely new set of gods. Instead, he incorporated deities already worshiped in Chinese folk religion into his growing religious system.

The Jade Emperor, however, was not central in early Taoism. He rose to prominence much later, especially during the Tang dynasty (618–907 CE), when he came to be seen as the supreme ruler of Heaven.

Taoism has two myths of the Jade Emperor's origins, but in both stories, he started out as a human. In one story, he was a soldier who fought and died in the Battle of Muve (1046 BCE), which overturned the Shang dynasty. The dead soldiers were in Heaven, receiving their rewards. A nobleman who had also died, Jiang Ziya, was appointing the soldiers to Heavenly positions for their bravery in battle. Only one position remained—the Jade Emperor—which Jiang Ziya wanted for himself.

Jiang Ziya pretended to be modest, waiting for the rest of the soldiers to recommend him, which they did. He humbly answered, "Deng lai," ("Wait a minute"), as if he needed to consider his worthiness. Amusingly, "Deng Lai" was the name of a brave soldier who had fought and died in the battle. When he heard "Deng lai," he thought Jiang Ziya was calling his name and stepped forward to receive his new appointment as Heaven's sovereign god.

In another Jade Emperor origin myth, the queen of the Kingdom of Miraculous Joy and Heavenly Lights had a dream about the philosopher Laozi, which led to her pregnancy. Her son eventually became king and ruled wisely, yet his goal was to cultivate Tao. He left for the Bright and Fragrant Cliffs to meditate and ultimately became an immortal who fought demons. When an army of formidable demons set out to take over Heaven, the king flew up to fight the terrifying chief demon. The king defeated the devil and became the Jade Emperor, Heaven's high god.

The Weaver Girl and the Cowherd

The Jade Emperor married **Xi Wangmu** (Queen Mother of the West), whom the Chinese had worshiped since the Shang dynasty. She was once a deity of death and disaster, portrayed with tiger teeth, but she transformed into a kinder goddess. The Jade Emperor and Xi Wangmu had many children, including a daughter named **Zhinu**, the "Weaver Girl." She spun the clouds and wove the sunsets and constellations.

One day, Zhinu used her magical robe to fly to Earth, where she went for a swim in a sparkling river. A humble yet handsome cowherd named **Niulang** saw her when he brought his cattle to drink. He picked up the exquisite robe she had left on the riverbank.

"Ai ya!" Zhinu wailed. "That's my robe! Leave it alone! I can't fly back to Heaven without it."

The handsome herder cocked his head. "Stay here with me. Let's get married."

Zhinu admired his striking good looks. While she treaded water, they chatted, and she liked Niulang's witty yet kind nature. She agreed to marry him and moved into his cottage, where they lived a simple yet happy life together. However, every once in a while, she got homesick for Heaven. She especially missed seeing her mother, father, sisters, and brothers.

One day while cleaning, she found her magic robe, which Niulang had hidden.

"Ah! I'll use my robe to visit my family. I can get to Heaven and back before Niulang comes home with the cows."

However, when she got to Heaven, her father was not pleased. "I heard you married a cowherd!" raved the Jade Emperor. "What were you thinking? You're a goddess!"

"I love him, Baba. We're happy together. We have two children."

"It isn't proper! I won't allow it! You must stay here in Heaven now!"

The Jade Emperor flung the Milky Way between Heaven and Earth, preventing Zhinu from flying back to her husband. Zhinu fell to the ground, weeping in despair. After a time, her father could not bear her distress any longer.

"All right, I will let you visit your mortal family, but only once a year! On the seventh day of the seventh lunar month, a flock of magpies will form a bridge over the Milky Way."

Weaver Girl crosses the Milky Way in a painting from the Summer Palace in Beijing [16]

Each year in autumn, Zhinu crossed the Milky Way to visit her earthly husband and children.

"Our hearts are united, even when we are separated," she whispered.

If one looks into the sky in the early fall, away from the city lights, the Milky Way is darkest in the middle. The Chinese interpreted this as Zhinu's magpie bridge from Heaven to Earth. In reality, it is a supermassive black hole called Sagittarius A*.

How Chang'e Became the Moon Goddess

Chang'e was a lovely young woman married to the famous archer, Hou Yi, whom we will learn more about in the next chapter. Because of his spectacular deeds in saving Earth, Xi Wangmu flew down from Heaven to thank Hou Yi. She handed him a small vial.

"This vial holds the Elixir of Life. If you drink half of it, you will become immortal. If you drink the entire vial, you will become a god."

Hou Yi stood there, holding the vial. What should he do? If he became a god, his wife would still be mortal. He knew the Jade Emperor disapproved of marriages between gods and humans. Yet, if he were immortal, his dear Chang'e would one day die. He could not imagine living an eternity without her.

Just at that moment, Chang'e walked in. He handed her the vial and told her what the Queen Mother of Heaven had told him. "I don't know what to do. Hold this for me. Put it somewhere safe while I go hunting."

Minutes after Hou Yi left, Peng Meng came into the house. He was Hou Yi's apprentice and had overheard what Xi Wangmu told Hou Yi when she gave him the vial. He startled Chang'e, who was holding her pet rabbit.

"Where is the vial?" he asked.

"What vial?" Chang'e inquired. She had never liked Peng Meng.

Peng Meng's face darkened. "You know what vial! The one the Queen Mother of Heaven gave Hou Yi! I was there and heard everything she said."

"I can't give it to you, Peng Meng."

Chang'e knew chaos would erupt if she gave the vial to Peng Meng. What if he became a god? He would stir up war in Heaven! She pulled the vial out of her sleeve, unplugged the cork, and swallowed its entire contents.

"No!" screamed Peng Meng, his face turning red.

For several seconds, nothing happened. Chang'e stood there, holding her rabbit, with the empty vial in her other hand. Then, her feet lifted off the floor. She gently floated out the window. Her maid was outside washing clothes and screamed when she saw Chang'e floating through the air.

"Chang'e! Chang'e! Come back! Don't leave us!"

Meanwhile, Peng Meng ran out of the house and down the road. No one ever saw him in the region again.

When Hou Yi came home that evening, his wife's maid was hysterical. "Chang'e! She floated out the window and into the sky!"

"Where? Where is she? Chang'e! Where are you? Don't leave me!"

Chang'e flies to the moon [17]

Night had fallen, and Hou Yi looked up at the moon. Why was it so bright?

"Ai ya! Look! On the moon! There's a rabbit on the moon! Chang'e must be up there on the moon."

Frantically, he turned to the maid. "Help me set up an altar here, where my wife can see it. Chang'e has become the moon goddess. She must be lonely up there by herself. We must burn incense and offer her fruit and little cakes to let her know we love her."

One version of the myth says that the Mother of the Moon, **Changxi**, permitted Chang'e and Hou Yi to reunite each year in the eighth lunar month. To this day, Chinese people honor Chang'e on "Moon Day" or Mid-Autumn Festival, held on the fifteenth day of the eighth lunar month (late September to early October). Families gather for a feast and light paper lanterns. They lay out offerings and burn incense on a little table outside for Chang'e on the moon. They eat mooncakes, heavy pastries with dense fillings like red bean paste, salted duck egg yolk, nuts, or seeds.

The Butterfly Lovers

This classic tale continues the theme of love and loss. It takes place during the Jin dynasty (266–420 CE). In those days, girls could not attend school, although a few received tutoring at home. Usually, only boys from wealthy families went to school. However, boys from poor families sometimes attended if their village collectively paid their tuition (this still happens in China today, as tuition is required for high school). The point of education beyond primary school was to prepare for the civil service examinations. If a student passed the examination, he qualified for an administrative position in the government.

Zhu Yingtai was an attractive, intelligent thirteen-year-old in a wealthy family in Zhejiang Province. She had learned to read and write, but she longed for more education, so she asked her father to send her to school.

"Why?" asked her father. "You have all the skills you need for a young woman. You cannot work in the government, so there is no reason to prepare for the exams."

"Yes, Baba, I know all that. But my heart longs for more. If I were a boy, I could study Confucian classics, history, poetry, and literature. I just want to learn these things."

"Yingtai, my dear, they won't let a girl into the school."

"I've thought it all out, Baba. I'll take my maid Xiao Qing with me. We'll both disguise ourselves as boys. We'll share a room at the boarding house near the school."

Yingtai's father reluctantly gave in. "Listen carefully, Yingtai. You can go, but I must arrange your marriage when you are sixteen. The law says girls have to be married by seventeen. If you aren't married, our local government will choose a husband for you, and neither of us wants that! So, you must return home in three years to prepare for marriage."

Yingtai hugged her father. "Thank you, Baba! Yes, I promise I'll return home when I'm sixteen, get married, and start having babies. I understand. Our country needs more people."

Yingtai and Xiao Qing excitedly prepared to leave. They learned to tie their hair in a touji bun on top of their heads, as the boys did. They dressed as boys and traveled to the city where the school was. On the way, they met a boy named Liang Shanbo, who was traveling to the same school, so they walked together, enjoying a lively conversation. At the school, Shanbo considered Yingtai his younger brother, calling her "Didi." Yingtai's feelings for Shanbo quickly grew into more than brotherly love, though. However, she did so well passing as a boy that Shanbo suspected nothing. They studied together every day, sometimes falling asleep on the same bed.

When she was sixteen, Yingtai's father wrote to her, asking her to come home, as it was time to prepare for marriage. He did not tell her he had already arranged her betrothal to a young man named Ma Wencai in a nearby town. With tears in her eyes, Yingtai told Shanbo that her father was asking her to come home. Shanbo offered to walk with her for the first eighteen miles of the journey. On the long walk, she kept giving Shanbo hints of her true identity, but he failed to catch on.

Finally, she said, "I have a beautiful younger sister at home. I think she would be the perfect wife for you. Come visit me, and I'll encourage my father to arrange a marriage."

Weeks later, when school was out, Shanbo traveled to visit Yingtai and meet her sister. However, he was shocked when Yingtai greeted him dressed as a young woman. "I'm a girl, Shanbo! I have always loved you. Please ask my father for my hand in marriage."

However, when Shanbo approached her father, he received sad news. "You seem like a fine young man, Shanbo, but I have already betrothed her to a boy named Ma Wencai. He's from a wealthy family in the next town. I cannot break the contract. They will marry in a year."

Shanbo stumbled out of the house, his eyes blurry with tears. He could not imagine life without Yingtai. His grief was so great that he could not eat and grew alarmingly thin. Knowing he would soon die, Shanbo told his servant, "Bury me near Yingtai's village, next to the road where she will travel to her wedding."

Yingtai had been resisting her marriage to Wencai, but when she heard Shanbo had died, she finally agreed to the wedding. "I ask only one thing. On my wedding day, let the procession pass by Shanbo's grave, so I can pay my respects."

On the day of her wedding, Yingtai dressed in a red wedding gown, and the women arranged her hair in elaborate braids and jewels. She sat in a sedan chair and was carried toward the nearby town of her fiancé, followed by a parade of friends and family playing music, lighting firecrackers, and carrying red banners proclaiming good luck to the new couple. When they reached the place where Shanbo was buried, Yingtai stepped down from her chair and knelt at his grave.

Suddenly, a windstorm blew, stirring up dust and breaking tree limbs. Everyone dashed for shelter except Yingtai. Then, lightning flashed, striking Shanbo's grave and breaking it open. Without hesitating, Yingtai jumped into the grave. With a clap of thunder, the grave closed back up. The wind stopped, the thunderclouds went away, and the sun came out. Yingtai's family and friends gathered at the roadside grave, shaken. Then, they saw two butterflies on the grave. They took wing, fluttering and circling each other, rising gently upward until they disappeared.

Roundup Activity: Thought Questions

1. What does the Weaver and Cowherd story reveal about the personalities of Zhinu and Niulang?

2. Why do you think Zhinu and Niulang's love story is still remembered today? What makes their story special?

3. If you were the Jade Emperor, would you have allowed Zhinu and Niulang to meet more than once a year? Explain why.

4. Do you think Chang'e made the right decision to drink the Elixir of Life to keep it from Peng Meng? Why or why not?

5. The myth of Chang'e is linked to the Mid-Autumn Festival, where people celebrate the full moon and family reunions. Why might a story about separation be so central to a festival celebrating togetherness?

6. What challenges would you face if you were a girl pretending to be a boy to attend school?

7. What do you think the final transformation of Yingtai and Shanbo into butterflies symbolizes?

8. Love, sacrifice, and separation are big themes in these stories. Have you ever had to sacrifice something important for someone you care about?

9. These myths are ancient but still touch our hearts. Can you think of a modern love story (from a movie, book, or real life) that reminds you of one of these tales?

10. Which of the three love stories did you like the best and why?

Chapter 6: The Sun Chaser: The Endurance of Hou Yi

This chapter recounts the legend of **Hou Yi**, the "Lord Archer" who saved the world by shooting down nine of the ten suns that scorched the earth. The chapter also explores the story of the **Jade Rabbit**, who lives on the moon with Chang'e, crafting the Elixir of Life. These myths weave together themes of heroism, love, sacrifice, and the acceptance of one's fate. They encourage us to reflect on the impact of our choices and the importance of cherishing the time we have.

The Hou Yi stories date to the Warring States Period (1046–256 BCE), a millennium before the Jade Emperor became a Chinese deity. The Taoists added the Jade Emperor to earlier folk tales featuring Hou Yi.

Hou Yi and the Mythical Beasts

Hou Yi and Chang'e were once immortals living with the Jade Emperor in his palace in Heaven. Hou Yi was incredibly strong. He carried a heavy bow made of tiger bone. He was the only one powerful enough to draw the bow. Hou Yi crafted his arrows from the tendons of a dragon. He used his bow to defend China from mythical beasts and celestial tyrants.

The Qin dynasty (221–206 BCE) book, *Huainanzi*, told of several savage creatures threatening the empire in the days of the legendary Emperor Yao (2356–2255 BCE). The Zaochi was a long-toothed, human-like monster living in the southern swamps, capturing and devouring people. Nine colossal children, who lived in the north, ran around spitting water on the cooking fires in people's courtyards. Dongting Lake, the flood basin of the Yangtze River, had an enormous Bashe snake lurking in its depths that swallowed entire elephants. (Yes, China had a subspecies of wild Asian elephants in that area until the Han dynasty.) Roaming the central plain was the Yayu, which had a dragon head and a panther's body. Its wails sounded like a human baby crying, luring people to their deaths. The Fengxi, which looked like a two-headed boar, terrorized the rural areas, destroying villages and devouring cattle. Hou Yi killed all these monsters, restoring order to China.

A sculpture of Hou Yi killing the Bashe serpent [18]

Hou Yi and the Ten Suns

In the days when Earth was young, the solar system had ten suns, the sons of the Jade Emperor and his second wife, Xihe, the sun goddess. The ten suns took turns rising in the morning, riding across the sky in a chariot, and setting in the evening.

Their father cautioned them, "Make sure only one of you is in the sky at a time. Otherwise, you will be too hot for Earth."

Despite his warning, the mischievous sons decided to do things differently one day. "Wouldn't it be fun for all of us to travel across the sky at once?"

And so they did. However, the heat of ten suns together brought a near-apocalypse. Rivers dried up, and the fish all died. The crops and forests burned, and the people suffered dreadfully. The Jade Emperor scolded his sons and told them to come out of the sky, but they were playing and laughing so hard that they did not hear him.

The Jade Emperor called for Hou Yi. "Go stop my ten foolish sons from destroying Earth!"

Hou Yi climbed a high mountain and tried to reason with the suns. "Please! Come out of the sky now! Come back to your father's palace. If you don't, I will have to shoot you!"

But they just laughed and stuck their tongues out at Hou Yi. "Mind your own business!" they shouted.

A Han dynasty etching of Hou Yi shooting the suns[19]

So, Hou Yi took his bow and arrows and shot each of the suns out of the sky, one by one. As the suns fell from the sky, they transformed into black crows with three legs. The tenth sun escaped and took shelter in a cave. With no suns, the world suddenly became cold and dark.

"Come out! Come out of the cave," begged the people of Earth.

At first, the tenth sun ignored them. He stayed in the cave with his hands over his ears. Finally, a rooster flew to the cave and loudly crowed, "Gege! (Brother). Come out!"

When he heard the rooster, the sun finally came out. That sun remained in the sky, setting each night and rising each day when the rooster crowed. He gave the proper amount of light and warmth to Earth. However, the Jade Emperor was furious that Hou Yi had shot nine of his sons, turning them into crows.

"I fixed the problem, as you commanded me to do," Hou Yi tried to explain.

Nevertheless, the Jade Emperor banished Hou Yi and Chang'e to Earth, and they lost their immortal status. That is when Xi Wangmu, the Jade Emperor's first wife, took matters into her own hands. She knew Hou Yi had done the right thing by shooting down the nine suns (they were not her sons, after all). She decided to restore Hou Yi's immortal status and flew down to Earth with the Elixir of Life. However, she brought only enough for one person, and that is where the trouble started.

Hou Yi Shoots Hebo and Takes His Wife Luoshen

Hebo ("Lord of the River") was the god of the Yellow River, northern China's most important waterway. Hebo's character was inseparable from the Yellow River itself. It could be benevolent and life-giving or a devastating life-snatching torrent, causing China great sorrow.

Hebo was also called Bing Yi ("Ice End"). He was once a man named Feng Yi who drowned while trying to curb an overwhelming flood. Impressed by his sacrifice, the Jade Emperor made him the god of the Yellow River. The Upper Yellow River freezes in the winter, and ice jams frequently cause disastrous floods. Feng Yi got the nickname "Ice End" or "Bing Yi" as a dark allusion to his troublesome side.

The *Cu Chi,* a collection of songs and poems from the Warring States Period, said the emperor sent Hou Yi to reform the people of Xia. The Xia region of China was along the Yellow River, where modern-day Henan Province is. Apparently, Hou Yi helped the people by driving out or subduing dragons and other animals.

Hou Yi shot Hebo in the left eye after he morphed into a white dragon and was drowning people with his floods. Hebo also received human sacrifices, especially young women. After shooting Hebo, Hou Yi stole his wife, Luoshen. She was the beautiful goddess of the Luo River, a tributary of the Yellow River. She symbolized unattainable love. Chinese poetry described her dancing gracefully on the riverbank.

Hebo, who was not actually killed, complained to the Supreme God about Hou Yi shooting him and stealing his wife. The Supreme God asked Hebo, "What were you doing when you got shot? Were you performing your duties? No! You were masquerading as a white dragon and creating chaos. Hou Yi did the right thing."

Hou Yi shoots Hebo and steals his wife [20]

The Jade Rabbit

The Jade Rabbit is the creature whose shape can be seen on the moon. One version of the Jade Rabbit story is that he accompanied Chang'e to the moon. However, another story says that the Jade Emperor sent him there for a special task. He needed someone to prepare the Elixir of Life, but felt that if he gave the task to humans, they would try to consume the magical concoction of immortality.

"I'll use an animal," he decided. "But which animal would best fit the task?"

To choose an animal, the Jade Emperor descended to Earth, disguised as a beggar, crying out for food. Three creatures approached him with concern: a fox, a monkey, and a rabbit. When they realized he was starving, they ran off to search for food. The fox caught a fish in a stream and brought it to the beggar. The monkey jumped around in the trees and returned with an assortment of fruit. The rabbit hopped around and could find nothing that a human could eat. He sadly returned to the beggar and found him roasting the fish over a fire and enjoying the fruit.

"I found nothing for the man to eat, so I'll give him myself!" The rabbit jumped into the fire.

"Ai ya!" screamed the beggar. "Don't kill yourself!"

The beggar instantly changed back into the Jade Emperor and snatched the rabbit from the fire.

"Rabbit, you are a noble and selfless creature. You care more about others than your own life. I am giving you the task of preparing the Elixir of Life. You will live on the moon, where the humans cannot disturb you or try to steal the elixir."

Roundup Activity: Thought Questions

1. Hou Yi killed multiple monsters to save civilization. What does this tell you about him?

2. Hou Yi shot down nine suns to save Earth. What's the bravest thing you've ever done or would like to do?

3. If the Jade Emperor told you to deal with the ten suns, how would you go about it?

4. Do you think it was right for the Jade Emperor to banish Hou Yi and Chang'e to Earth? What does this tell you about the Jade Emperor?

5. If you were Chang'e, how would you feel about the Jade Emperor banishing you to Earth for something your husband did?

6. Why do you think Xi Wangmu only gave enough of the Elixir of Life for Hou Yi and not Chang'e?

7. Do you consider Hou Yi a hero, a tragic figure, or a bully? Explain your answer.

8. Chang'e ended up on the moon because of the elixir. If you could live anywhere in the universe, where would it be and why?

9. The Jade Rabbit is known for its sacrifice. What's the biggest thing you've ever given up for someone else?

10. Since the beggar was roasting fish and eating fruit when the rabbit returned, do you think it was over the top for the rabbit to sacrifice himself? What does this tell you about the Chinese value of sacrifice for a guest?

Chapter 7: The Dragon's Pearl: Rulers of Rivers and Seas

This chapter dives into the mystical world of dragons, the guardians of China's rivers and seas. It begins with the myth of the dragon and his pearl, which has the power to control the weather. This tale intertwines with the story of Yu the Great, who tamed the Great Flood that devastated the Yellow River region. Next, the chapter unfolds the story of the dragon, the phoenix, and a resplendent pearl. The chapter also unwraps Buddhist myths surrounding Guanyin and Longnu in the tale of the Dragon King's daughter. These narratives combine to paint a picture of water's crucial role in Chinese mythology and history, symbolizing life, power, and change.

The Dragon and His Pearl

In ancient times, a drought in the Sichuan region left people hungry and thirsty. China's emperor was corrupt, interested only in what he could get from his people. He did nothing to end their suffering.

During the famine, Nie Lang, a young teen, tried to support himself and his widowed mother by selling grass as feed for animals. From his tiny profit, he bought a small amount of rice each day that kept him and his mother from starving. However, as the sun grew hotter and the drought continued, the grass dried up.

Nie Lang looked desperately at his mother, wasting away from malnutrition. "Where can I find grass?" he thought to himself.

He hiked to a distant mountain and climbed to its peak, where he scanned the surrounding countryside, hoping to see green grass somewhere. He plunged into despair when he saw nothing but brown barrenness. A sudden movement caught his attention—a plump rabbit! He chased after the rabbit, hoping to catch it for food. However, the rabbit led him to a small field of lush green grass.

"Thank you, rabbit!" Nie Lang said, tears streaming down his cheeks. "I'm sorry that I wanted to eat you!"

Nie Lang gathered a large bundle of grass, then hiked to the marketplace to sell it. He got an excellent price, enough to buy his mother an enormous meal—not just rice but also vegetables and meat. The next day, he hiked back to the same place and found plenty of grass. It was as if he had never harvested any.

"Wow!" he exclaimed. "Look at all this grass!"

He harvested more grass, trudged the long distance to the marketplace, sold the grass, and bought another nourishing meal for his mother and himself. Day after day, he traveled to the mountain pasture to cut grass to sell. He was thrilled to have food for his mother, but the mountain was miles from his home.

"I think I'll dig up some of this grass and plant it by our house. That way I won't have to walk so far every day."

While digging up the sod, he found an enormous, gleaming pearl. He rushed home with the sod and pearl. "Ma! Look at this pearl! Think how much I can get if I sell it!"

"No, son," his mother replied. Let's keep it. Its beauty will bless us."

His mother tucked the pearl away in an empty rice bag, while Nie Lang went outside to plant the sod. However, when he went outside the next morning, the grass he had planted had wilted. He collapsed to the ground, weeping.

Suddenly, he heard his mother calling him. "Nie Lang! Come quickly!"

He rushed inside the cottage to find his mother holding a full rice bag, trembling with joy.

"Look! The bag is full of rice!"

"Oh, Ma! We have enough for ourselves and our neighbors! We can feed the entire village!"

Days passed, and everyone in the village had enough to eat. Nie Lang mused, "This pearl blesses everything around it!"

Eventually, the emperor heard about the prospering village. He sent his soldiers to find out the secret. "Sichuan is in the middle of a drought. Find out what is going on in that village!"

When the soldiers arrived and interrogated the people, the villagers only knew that it had to do with Nie Lang and his mother. So, they barged into Nie Lang's cottage, demanding the truth. Nie Lang and his mother stayed silent, so they tore apart the cottage until his mother finally told them about the pearl. At that moment, Nie Lang popped the pearl into his mouth to keep it from the soldiers.

However, Nie Lang accidentally swallowed the pearl. "Ai ya! I'm thirsty! And hot! I'm burning inside!"

He raced to the river, scooping up and drinking the tiny trickle of muddy water. At that moment, thunder rumbled, and lightning flashed as rain clouds rolled in. A deluge fell from the sky, soaking the land and filling the river. The villagers cheered as the soldiers stood paralyzed with astonishment.

But Nie Lang's mother screamed, tears flowing from her face. "Wow! Nie Lang has turned into a dragon!"

Nie Lang was covered in glistening green scales and had a long, serpentine tail. He extended his enormous wings and rose into the sky.

"Goodbye, dear son!" his mother wept. "Thank you for saving our land!"

A Qing dynasty ceramic with a dragon and a flaming pearl [21]

Yu, the Dragon Engineer

In this story, the people had the opposite problem. Instead of a drought, the towns and villages in the Yellow River Valley had suffered a prolonged flood at the beginning of the Xia dynasty (2070–1600 BCE). China did not yet have writing, but stories of the catastrophic, years-long flood were written centuries later. Recent findings show the flood was not simply mythological. A landslide triggered by an earthquake plugged up the Yellow River in the Jishi Gorge.[i]

King Yao went to the Four Mountains, asking what to do. "Give your cousin Gun the job of controlling the flood," they told him.

Gun went to work building dams. However, the unrelenting flood collapsed the dams. This cycle continued for nine years. Finally, Gun snuck into Heaven and stole some *xirang* or divine soil that expanded when wet. His xirang dams finally controlled the flooding. Unfortunately, the Supreme God discovered his dirt was missing.

---

[i] Qinglong Wu, et al., "Outburst Flood at 1920 BCE Supports Historicity of China's Great Flood and the Xia Dynasty," *Science* 353, no. 6299 (2016): 579-582, 10.1126/science.aaf084 https://www.science.org/doi/10.1126/science.aaf0842

"Kill Gun!" he ordered in a fury. "I'm taking my xirang back!"

Now, Gun was dead, and with the xirang dams destroyed, the deadly flooding resumed.

However, something odd happened with Gun's body. It did not decompose. Instead, Yu emerged from his body as a dragon, charging out of the tomb three years after his father died. Yu the Engineer immediately set to work controlling the floods. Rather than damming the rivers, he built multiple channels to drain them into the sea. This was a daunting task as mountains stood in the way. Yu opted to tunnel through Jishi Mountain. Then, he split Longmen Mountain, calling the opening the "Dragon Gate." Thirteen years later, he had successfully drained the floodwater and became the first emperor of the Xia dynasty.

Silk dragon tapestry[22]

Dragon, Phoenix, and the Resplendent Pearl

In Chinese mythology, the dragon and phoenix were sometimes seen as a couple, with artwork of the pair dating to over five thousand years ago. The Chinese phoenix, called Fenghuang, was unlike the phoenix in Western mythology, which went through cycles of death and rebirth from its ashes. The Chinese phoenix was immortal.

In this myth, Dragon was swimming in a river one day while Phoenix looked on from a tree branch. Dragon asked Phoenix where the river went, and she told him it ran to the sea.

"Let's fly there!" Dragon said eagerly, so they did.

The couple arrived at the seashore as the sun set, bathing everything in a golden-red glow.

"This is incredible!" breathed Dragon. "I want to fly over the sea! Let's do that tomorrow."

So, the next morning, they soared over the sea until they came to a little island, where they flew down to take a rest. Dragon looked around approvingly at the white sand and swaying palm trees. A sparkling blue lake with a waterfall lay in the middle of the island.

"This is the most beautiful place in the world!" Dragon exclaimed.

Phoenix nodded as she gazed at the lake. Then, she noticed something. "Dragon, what is that on the lake bottom? It's shining!"

"I'll find out," said Dragon, diving in. He came back to the surface holding a large, radiant pearl. "Phoenix, it's glowing!"

"Yes, it is," came a voice from below.

The two looked down to see a crab waving a claw. He told them, "That is a magic pearl. Put it back now! It is what keeps this island so pristine and lovely. It symbolizes harmony, prosperity, and eternal life. The plants that grow near this pearl never die."

Dragon placed the pearl back on the lake bottom. "Phoenix, we love this place. Why don't we just stay here forever and protect this priceless pearl?"

And so, the couple remained on the island as guardians of the magic pearl. However, this was when the world was young, before the goddess Xi Wangmu had reformed into a benevolent deity. She was still the untamed, unhinged goddess of chaos and calamity, with wild, disheveled hair. Xi Wangmu had heard about the glowing pearl and wanted it for herself. So, she sent her guard to get it. The guard snuck down to the island during midday nap time and stole the pearl while Dragon and Phoenix slept. When they awakened, they were horrified to find the pearl missing. They flew up into the air, scouring the world for the resplendent pearl.

Finally, they discovered Xi Wangmu had stolen the priceless pearl. In a celestial mid-air battle, the pearl fell to the ground. Lightning flashed, and the earth quaked as the pearl melted and formed a glistening emerald lake. Instantly, Dragon and Phoenix transformed themselves into mountains to guard the mystical lake for eternity.

A Ming dynasty plate with a phoenix and a dragon [23]

The Dragon King's Daughter

Longnu was the daughter of Sagara, the Dragon King, who lived in a palace at the bottom of the sea. When she was very young, Longnu often took the form of a little snake when she wanted to leave the sea and roam the land. One day, someone captured her and put her into a bottle, and she had to wait for rescue. After what seemed like an eternity, Red Boy came walking through the forest. He was the child of a demon and had once been a fire-breathing monster. However, he had reformed and was now studying Buddhism under the Bodhisattva Guanyin.

As Red Boy approached, he heard what sounded like a little girl crying. He looked down to see a tiny snake in a bottle.

"Help me!" cried the snake.

Red Boy popped the cork out and released the little snake, but Longnu suddenly morphed into a dragon. "Thank you! Now, I'm going to eat you! I'm starving!"

"You can't eat me!" wailed Red Boy. "I just freed you!"

"I'm a dragon. It's what we do."

"That's unjust! You can't eat your rescuer!"

"Oh, all right," sighed Longnu. "Let's ask the first three beings who come by and let them judge."

The first creature that came down the forest path was a water buffalo. He was not a fan of people because they had mistreated him, so he had no qualms about Longnu eating Red Boy.

"Well, I'm not really a boy. I was born a monster," Red Boy tried to explain, but it did not help his case.

Next, a Taoist priest came along, who believed in letting nature take its course. He was uninterested in rescuing Red Boy. Finally, a little girl came walking down the path.

"Yes, you can eat the boy, but first, show me how you fit in that tiny bottle."

Longnu morphed back from a dragon into a little snake and slithered into the bottle. The girl swiftly corked the bottle, trapping Longnu. Then, the child transformed into her true identity, Guanyin.

"If you want to be set free, you must study Buddhist principles with me," Guanyin sternly told Longnu.

Longnu became a student of Guanyin and studied so diligently that by the time she was eight years old, she was close to achieving Buddhahood. Siddhartha Gautama, the founder of Buddhism in India, was the first Buddha. However, anyone who had detached themselves from the world and attained enlightenment could enter the state of freedom called Nirvana. Guanyin was a bodhisattva, a person who reached enlightenment but delayed Nirvana to teach others.

Manjushri was another bodhisattva. He admired Longnu's swift journey toward enlightenment. As Longnu climbed the mountain to Vulture Peak, the Buddha's retreat, he pointed her out to the other disciples. "She's only a little girl, but she is wise and has mastered everything!"

One disciple, Sariputra, sneered at Longnu. "Do you think you can achieve 'the Way' so quickly? You are only a child—worse yet, you're a girl! How can you understand such deep things? And a dragon! Whoever heard of a dragon achieving Buddhahood?"

Manjushri coughed. "Well, actually, the *Lotus Sutra* says all creatures can attain enlightenment. Even females. Or, I suppose, dragons, for that matter. All beings possess Buddha-nature."

Sariputra scoffed. "She's only eight years old. How can she learn everything so fast?"

Longnu ignored Sariputra and the others. She was carrying the Dragon King's priceless pearl. Her father's jewel represented spiritual knowledge and immense power. She held it up to the sky as an offering to the Buddha, and he accepted it. Instantly, she was transported to the Pure Land as a Buddha, where she sat on a jeweled lotus.

Roundup Activity: Thought Questions

1. Dragons are scary creatures in other cultures, but they are powerful and respected in Chinese mythology. Why do you think that is?

2. What does Nie Lang's story tell you about the Chinese respect and care for their parents?

3. Nie Lang and his mother shared their rice with all the villagers. What does this imply about the importance of community in China? Would you do the same thing?

4. Yu the Engineer worked hard to control the floods. Can you think of a time when you put a lot of energy into a project? What was it, and how did it turn out?

5. Yu used a different approach to control the floods than his father, Gun. Have you ever had to try a different way to solve a problem?

6. In the resplendent pearl story, Dragon had a happy-go-lucky, adventurous nature, but he also took responsibility seriously. Do either of these describe you? Explain.

7. If you had a magical pearl, what would you do with it?

8. In the Red Boy and Little Snake story, neither the snake nor the little girl is what they seem. What does this say about our complex natures?

9. Both Red Boy and Longnu reformed their evil ways. Do you think turning a new leaf is possible for anybody?

10. In most versions of Longnu's story, she transforms into a man after offering the pearl to Buddha and before she attains Buddhahood. What are your thoughts on this?

Chapter 8: The Monkey King's Rebellion: Journey to the West

This chapter spotlights Sun Wukong, the rebel Monkey King, who traveled as the monk Tripitaka's bodyguard on a perilous journey to India to retrieve Buddhist scripture. Adding to the mix is Zhu Bajie, a partially reformed pig demon with a good heart but constant failings. Zhu Bajie and the cheeky Monkey King provide comic relief and lessons on redemption and humility.

These stories form the core of the Qing dynasty's *Journey to the West*, which is based on older myths. As one of China's four famous classical novels, it offers themes of adventure, loyalty, and enlightenment. They challenge us to think about the value of friendship, knowledge, and personal growth.

An Unusual Birth

Near the beginning of time, after Gonggong broke the sky, and Nuwa was mending it, she dropped one of her colored stones. It fell on the mythical Mount Huaguo, where it lay for millennia, bathed in the light of the sun and moon. Eventually, the Bodhisattva Guanyin climbed to the mountaintop to meditate, imbuing the stone with her spiritual energy.

Shortly after Guanyin left, the stone cracked open, hatching a stone macaque, later named Sun Wukong by a powerful sage. The name meant "monkey awakened to emptiness," alluding to his life journey as a chaotic, untamed monkey who finally "emptied" himself to achieve understanding and wisdom.

When Sun Wukong first hatched, he was a stone that gradually came to life. First, he opened his eyes, shooting two gold beams toward Heaven, which startled the Jade Emperor.

"Wow! Where did those lights come from? Go down to Mount Huaguo and find out what is going on," he ordered his nephew, Erlang Shen, a powerful warrior god who had a third, all-seeing eye.

Meanwhile, the newborn stone monkey was softening and morphing into a living creature. By the time Erlang Shen had traveled from Heaven to Mount Huaguo, Sun Wukong had learned how to move around. He was about halfway down the mountain, playing with some newfound monkey friends in a stream.

"It's nothing. Just an ordinary monkey," Erlang Shen reported to the Jade Emperor.

Sun Wukong was rapidly learning about his surroundings and asked his monkey friends, "Where does this stream begin?"

"Well, water travels downhill, so it must come from the top of the mountain," the oldest monkey answered.

"It couldn't come from the very top because that's where I hatched," mused Wukong.

The oldest monkey nodded. "If you follow the stream up the mountain, you will find its source."

Wukong sprang up. "Ah! Let's do that right now!"

He swung from tree to tree, following the stream uphill, with the other monkeys right behind him. When they came to a waterfall near the mountaintop, the oldest monkey said, "That's where the stream flows out of the mountain!" He looked at Sun Wukong and cocked his head. "Whoever passes through that waterfall will be our king!"

Sun Wukong looked around, but the other monkeys were too nervous to go through the waterfall. So, he plunged through and immediately called out to the other monkeys. "Everyone! I found a cave! Come on through!"

The other monkeys gathered their courage and plowed through the waterfall to join him in the cave.

"This is the Water-Curtain Cave! We can live here safely," Sun Wukong announced. "And I'm now your Handsome Monkey King!"

Monkey King in a Chinese opera[24]

Journey to Immortality

Not long afterward, the oldest monkey died. Monkey King wept, as he had grown to love him. He depended on his friend's experience and wisdom. Monkey King knew nothing about death, which sent him on a new quest. "How can I conquer death?"

He descended from the mountain, looking for an immortal to teach him how to live forever. He finally arrived at a temple where an enlightened sage named Puti Zushi taught him the secrets of immortality through the **seventy-two earthly transformations**. Sun Wukong also learned martial arts and how to use supernatural powers, like changing into other creatures or traveling miles in one leap.

The Jade Emperor was furious when he learned Monkey King had achieved immortality and become a mighty martial arts warrior. "Heaven knows what will happen with him running around loose on Earth. Bring him up here where I can monitor him!"

Monkey King excitedly arrived in Heaven, where the Jade Emperor announced, "I'm making you Keeper of the Heavenly Horses."

Monkey King proudly went to work caring for Heaven's horses until he discovered it was the lowest position in Heaven. "Ai ya! I'm shoveling manure up here when I could be a king down there!"

Sun Wukong's Staff

Sun Wukong returned to his mountain to discover his monkeys were in trouble. The Demon King of Confusion had been kidnapping and enslaving them. Sun Wukong killed the Demon King and freed his monkeys. He then taught them martial arts and armed them with weapons so they could defend themselves. The process reminded him that he needed a formidable weapon for himself.

"Puti Zushi spent a decade teaching me how to fight with a staff. Yet, I have no special staff. I need to find one!"

In his search for a staff, Monkey King learned that the Dragon King had an awesome weapon collection. So, he traveled to the Dragon King's palace at the bottom of the sea and pushed his way in.

The Dragon King furrowed his brow and blew smoke from his nostrils. "I know who you are! You're that troublesome monkey that got kicked out of Heaven."

"I did not get kicked out! I left on my own. It's better to be a king on Earth than shoveling horse manure in Heaven!"

The Dragon King laughed. He was no fan of the Jade Emperor. "Why are you here?"

"As a master of martial arts, I need a special staff to put my skills to the fullest use. I must protect my monkeys from the demons."

"You came to the right person," the Dragon King boasted. "I have more weapons than any king on Earth."

He showed Sun Wukong his vast weapon collection, yet nothing caught Monkey King's interest. None carried the power matching his specialized martial arts skills called "Hou Qian" (Monkey Fist) or "Monkey Kung Fu."

Ai Chun, the Dragon King's wife, cleared her throat. "Show him the Ruyi Jingu Bang."

"That's not a weapon!" the Dragon King answered, puzzled. Yu the Engineer had used the Ruyi Jingu Bang to measure water when ending the Great Flood. It was an iron rod that magically expanded or shrank as needed.

"I've seen it sending off radiant light in the past few days. It is as if it is trying to tell us something."

They brought the magical staff to Sun Wukong. As soon as it came near him, it began glowing. He reached out to take hold of it, and it shrank or grew, depending on his kung fu moves.

"That rod is meant for you!" the Dragon King said, smiling.

Sun Wukong and his Ruyi Jingu Bang in a Chinese opera [25]

Rebel in Heaven

"Ai ya!" the Jade Emperor fumed. "Now Monkey King has the Ruyi Jingu Bang! That monkey is already wreaking havoc! He's wiped his name out of the Book of Life and Death!"

This book recorded the birth, death, and lifespan of all living creatures on the earth, so by erasing his name, Sun Wukong ensured his immortality. When the Jade Emperor sent his celestial soldiers to arrest Monkey King, Sun Wukong used his unparalleled martial arts skills and his Ruyi Jingu Bang to beat them.

The Jade Emperor decided to take a different approach and politely invited Sun Wukong to Heaven for a new position. He would be Guardian of the Heavenly Peach Orchard. When Monkey King accepted, the Jade Emperor breathed a sigh of relief. "Keep your friends close and your enemies closer!"

Before long, the misbehaving Monkey King was creating chaos in Heaven, exasperating the Jade Emperor. His soldiers could not capture the cheeky macaque because his kung fu skills were too powerful. Sun Wukong was immortal, so no one could kill him. "I am the Great Sage! Heaven's equal!" the monkey roared.

The Jade Emperor sent word to Vulture Peak in India, asking the Buddha for help in subduing the saucy monkey. The story takes an interesting twist by shifting from Taoist tradition to Buddhism. When the Buddha arrived in Heaven, Monkey King impulsively leaped between him and the Jade Emperor.

"I'm stronger than anyone in Heaven!" Sun Wukong bragged. "I should be the Jade Emperor!"

The Jade Emperor's face turned crimson, but the Buddha smiled slightly and leaned toward Monkey King. "I've heard you've achieved the Cloud Somersault."

"Yes! I can travel thirty-four thousand miles in a single leap!"

"Can you? Well, if you can leap out of my palm, you can be the Jade Emperor!"

Sun Wukong laughed and performed the Cloud Somersault, throwing himself to what he thought was the edge of the universe. Five tall pillars stood before him.

"I'll mark them, so everyone will know I was here!"

He wrote "Old Sun was here" on one pillar and peed on another. Then, he somersaulted back, only to discover he had never left the Buddha's hand. The pillars had been the Buddha's fingers! Sun Wukong turned red when he saw one finger with his graffiti on it and another reeking of his urine. The Buddha cast him to Earth, covering him with a mountain of rocks, leaving only his hands and head sticking out.

"When you learn patience and humility, I will release you."

To India and Back

In the 7th century, a Chinese monk named Xuanzang made a sixteen-year pilgrimage to India to collect Buddhist scriptures. A monk in the *Journey to the West*, called Tripitaka or Tang Sanzang, is based on this real-life monk. At the time Tripitaka was ready to leave on his travels, Monkey King had been stuck under the mountain for five hundred years. He heard Guanyin was gathering pilgrims to travel to India with Tripitaka. She especially needed bodyguards, as the trip was dangerous, with bandits and demons ready to leap on their prey.

Sun Wukong sent a message to Guanyin. "I'm the world's greatest fighter. If you release me from this mountain, I will faithfully guard Tripitaka on his journey west."

Guanyin knew about Monkey King's terrible nature, but she believed no one was beyond redemption. She also knew that Sun Wukong really was the

Xuanzang on his way to India[26]

world's most formidable warrior. She let him out from under the mountain to guard the monk, but she gave Tripitaka a magic golden crown.

"Give that to Sun Wukong to wear on his head. It's so beautiful that he won't be able to resist it. Once he puts it on, he can never take it off. If he misbehaves, chant this spell over him. The circlet will squeeze his head, giving him an unbearable headache. He must learn that Buddhism requires restraint if he is to be a pilgrim."

Guanyin also knew that, despite Monkey King's superpowers, he still needed protection from the dangers ahead. She gave him three hairs. "Use one of these hairs if you find yourself in an inescapable situation. One hair will shapeshift you into a different form so you can get away."

Sun Wukong joined Tripitaka along with three other bodyguards: Pigsy (Zhu Bajie), Sandy (Sha Wujing), and White Dragon Horse (Bai Long Ma). Like Monkey King, they were all atoning for past sins.

After five hundred years of imprisonment, Sun Wukong was ready to prove himself a worthy warrior. It was not about him and his pride this time. It was about protecting the monk in the demon-infested, windswept deserts and the treacherous, snow-covered Himalaya Mountains. The demons believed they would become immortal if they could catch and eat Tripitaka.

Monkey King's traveling companion Pigsy (Zhu Bajie) had a human body and a pig head. He had always been a glutton and a womanizer. He tried to seduce Chang'e on the one day of the year she could travel from the moon to be with her husband, Hou Ji. The gods thought that was gross, so they gave him a pig's head. For Pigsy, overcoming temptation was a struggle.

Pigsy's self-indulgent and lazy lifestyle flew in the face of Mahayana Buddhism, which emphasized detachment from earthly pleasures, letting go of cravings, and not allowing desire to control. Buddhists believed strict self-discipline led to peace, clear thinking, and freedom from suffering. Tripitaka was a hardcore ascetic who considered worldly comforts a distraction. Pigsy's struggle against Buddhism's "five hindrances" (gluttony, laziness, sensual desire, ill will, and doubt about the path) represents the human battle between temptation and virtue. Despite his shortcomings, Pigsy brought formidable martial arts skills to his new role as Tripitaka's bodyguard. He could ride on clouds, cause earthquakes, and change day to night.

Another bodyguard, Sandy (Sha Wujing), got his name because he once lived in quicksand as a blue-skinned, red-bearded, man-eating beast. In an earlier life, he had been Heaven's General until he committed the crime of breaking a jade goblet at Wangmu's annual Peach Banquet of Immortality. The Jade Emperor beat him and banished him to Earth, where Sandy wore a necklace of his victims' skulls and carried a magic golden staff called "Monster-subduing Precious Rod."

Guanyin converted Sandy to Buddhism and recruited him as another bodyguard for Tripitaka. However, when he met Monkey King and Pigsy, they took one look at his skull necklace and mistook him for a demon. Pigsy and Sandy fought each other in a fierce underwater battle in the river until Guanyin intervened.

The monk Tripitaka rode the White Dragon Horse, who had once been a dragon. His father was the Dragon King of the West (brother of the Dragon King who gave Monkey King his special rod). The dragon breathed fire one day, accidentally burning the Jade Emperor's priceless pearl. The Jade Emperor wanted to kill him, but Guanyin convinced the chief god to let the dragon live as a white horse for Tripitaka to ride.

Monkey King, Tripitaka riding White Dragon Horse, Pigsy, and Sandy on the pilgrimage to India. Painting from Beijing's Summer Palace.[27]

Many demons tried to capture and eat Tripitaka, hoping to gain immortality. His bodyguards had to fend them off. "Lady White Bone" was a Cadaver Demon who shapeshifted into a beautiful princess, hoping Tripitaka would let her get near enough to kill him. However, Sun Wukong recognized her true identity and struck her with his Ruyi Jingu Bang staff. She then changed into an old lady, but Monkey King recognized her and hit her again. The third time, she transformed into an old man. This time, Sun Wukong killed the demon.

Not realizing all these people were the same demon, Tripitaka looked on in disbelief, thinking that Monkey King was attacking and killing ordinary people. The monk told Sun Wukong to leave, and Monkey King returned to his monkeys on top of Mount Huaguo.

After Sun Wukong left, the Yellow Robe Demon captured Tripitaka and held him captive. This demon had once been a star in Heaven but had been banished. Pigsy, Sandy, and the White Dragon Horse fought the demon. After being injured, the horse whinnied, "Pigsy! Go back to China and get Sun Wukong!"

"Monkey King!" yelled Pigsy when he reached Mount Huaguo. "Come with me now! The Yellow Robe Demon has imprisoned Tripitaka and will eat him!"

"That's not my business," grumbled Sun Wukong. "He shouldn't have banished me."

"I know, Monkey King, but have you heard what that demon has been saying about you? He says you've grown old and too weak to fight him."

"What! Me? I can't grow old. I'm immortal!" Sun Wukong growled. "I'll show that demon a thing or two. He'll find out just how weak I am!"

Monkey King used the Cloud Somersault and vaulted back to the border of China and India in seconds, confronting the demon at his cave. Although they were evenly matched in power, Sun Wukong gradually got the upper hand through his skills. Finally, the demon (Kui Mulang) retreated into his cave and blocked the entrance. Monkey King flew up to Heaven to get help from the Jade Emperor, who sent down celestial beings to lure the demon out of his cave. The demon surrendered and flew back to Heaven, where the Jade Emperor punished him by making him tend Heaven's furnace. However, the Jade Emperor later released Kui Mulang and sent him to assist Monkey King.

After many spine-chilling adventures, the pilgrims finally reached Vulture Peak in India, where the scriptures were kept at Thunderclap Monastery. Tripitaka, Sun Wukong, and his fellow pilgrims returned home to China with the sacred scrolls.

Roundup Activity: Thought Questions

1. If you could have any of Monkey King's powers, which one would you choose and why?

2. Tripitaka's journey was full of dangers. What's the longest journey you've ever been on, and what did you learn from it?

3. Zhu Bajie often messes up but tries to do right. Can you relate to making mistakes and trying to fix them? How?

4. *Journey to the West* is full of lessons. What do you think is the most important lesson from these stories?

5. Imagine you're on a quest with Monkey King and his friends. What role would you want in the group, and why?

6. Monkey King starts as a mischievous, power-hungry figure who causes chaos in Heaven. What traits make him a hero despite his rebellious nature?

7. Guanyin is the Bodhisattva of Compassion. Do her actions, such as giving the tight-fitting golden headband to control Sun Wukong, always seem "compassionate" in a conventional sense?

8. Do you think it was right for Tripitaka to send Monkey King home for killing the demons in disguise? Have you ever jumped to a conclusion about someone without having all the facts?

9. What are three positive character traits of Monkey King? Which do you think is the most important?

10. What are three negative character traits of Monkey King? Do you struggle with any of these?

Chapter 9: The Lantern Festival: A Tale of Reunion and Light

This chapter explores the **Lantern Festival**, which marks the end of Chinese New Year festivities. It focuses on reunion, light, and hope. The Chinese celebrate this festival on the fifteenth day of the lunar calendar's first month (February or early March). During this festival, red lanterns decorate the streets, bringing good luck and dispelling demons.

One myth linked to the festival is Yinglong, the Winged Dragon, who fought against evil spirits. Dragon dances are performed in Yinglong's honor. Although the Jade Rabbit is associated more with the Mid-Autumn Festival, he symbolizes longevity because he mixes the Elixir of Life on the moon. Chinese people create rabbit-shaped lanterns and offer sacrifices during the Lantern Festival to honor the Jade Rabbit and ensure long life and favorable fortune in the coming year.

Other myths explored in this chapter are the Jade Emperor's crane, the taming of the Nian monster, and the homesick maid. These stories explore why Chinese communities worldwide celebrate the Lantern Festival to this day. These tales highlight the festival's themes of community, joy, and the triumph of good over evil. The Lantern Festival fosters a sense of belonging and the importance of coming together to celebrate life, community, and family.

Yinglong the Winged Dragon

Yinglong is connected to Huangdi, the legendary first emperor who introduced civilization to China. With a massive wingspan, Yinglong was one of the world's oldest dragons. He took three thousand years to grow into an adult from a tiny water snake.

Yinglong the Winged Dragon assisted Emperor Huangdi in his battle against Chiyou's demon tribe of eighty-one brothers, each of whom had eight arms and four eyes and carried invincible lances. Chiyou himself had a bull's head and a human body. The winged dragon could control the rain, allowing him to summon a flood that devastated the demon army. He also brought rainfall for the farmers' crops.

Chiyou had once served Emperor Huangdi as his war god. However, he rebelled and allied with Fengbo, the wind god, and Yushi, the rain god. Yushi had more control over the rain than Yinglong, so the demon army was winning the battle until Emperor Huangdi's daughter Ba got involved. Ba controlled lightning and sent lightning strikes that broke up the storms Yushi and Fengbo had conjured. Yinglong used his fangs and tail to attack the enemy. Together, Ba and Yinglong defeated the demonic army, and Huangdi killed Chiyou.

Yinglong features in Lantern Festival celebrations in lantern displays and performances that bring dragons and other mythical creatures to life. In the dragon dances, Yinglong represents power, magic, and China's ancient mythology.

Yinglong and Huangdi sculpture at the Wuhan Dayu Cultural Garden in Wuhan, China[28]

The Jade Emperor's Crane

This myth, which explains how the Lantern Festival started, is about a crane that belonged to the Jade Emperor. Both the red-crowned crane and the black-necked crane carry religious symbolism in East Asia. These birds live at least thirty years; some even live to be eighty years old. Because of this, they represent long life. They also symbolize purity because of their white color. Many Chinese considered them messengers from Heaven. Chinese artwork sometimes shows sages and immortals riding cranes.

In this myth, the Jade Emperor had a treasured crane living in his palace garden in Heaven. One day, it flew to Earth, curious about the world. Unfortunately, it landed near a village where the people thought it was just an ordinary bird. The villagers feared he might destroy their crops, so they killed him.

When he heard about this, the Jade Emperor erupted in fury. "On the fifteenth day of the first lunar month, I will consume this village with fire!"

One of the Jade Emperor's daughters overheard his proclamation and flew down to Earth to warn the people in the village. The villagers gathered, trying to think of some way to avoid the Jade Emperor's wrath. They went to an insightful sage for advice. The sage meditated for a while, then nodded and smiled.

"The Jade Emperor will not burn your village if he thinks it's already on fire. Beginning with the third day before the appointed time of the holocaust, build bonfires in every street in town, and set them aflame. Keep them burning throughout the fifteenth day of the first lunar month. Also, hang red lanterns everywhere and light them. Set fireworks and firecrackers off on the fifteenth day. Make lots of noise and smoke!"

The villagers did everything that the sage advised. The Jade Emperor's soldiers arrived on the appointed day, but as they approached the village, they saw it covered with black smoke and flames leaping up in places. They heard the fireworks and thought they were explosions. The red lanterns made the village glow red.

"Some enemy force has attacked and burned them!" the Heavenly army remarked. "There's nothing left for us to do here!"

The celestial forces flew back to Heaven as the villagers laughed and danced with joy. They were saved! Every year, they celebrated escaping

Heaven's wrath. The festivities caught on and are celebrated throughout China to this day, with fireworks, firecrackers, red lanterns, and bonfires. The beat of drums, gongs, and cymbals announces the lion and dragon dances. Families gather in their ancestral villages, and everyone enjoys tangyuan, sweet or savory glutinous rice dumplings.

The round *denglong,* or red lanterns, made from paper or silk, highlight the cultural pride and joy of the season. Hung outside homes, along streets, and in public squares, the lanterns have intricate gold writing and designs, many with symbolic meanings. Some red lanterns have riddles written on them, and people enjoy solving them. Today, the lantern displays are supplemented with high-tech LED displays. The lanterns bring luck, prosperity, and protection from evil in the coming year. Some lanterns, with a flame inside them, are released over bodies of water, symbolizing troubles floating away as the New Year begins.

Chinese Lanterns [29]

Hongjun Laozu Tames the Nian Monster

In Chinese, the word *nian* means "year." However, "nian" was also the name of a terrifying mythical beast. Its name first appeared on oracle bones in the Shang dynasty (1600–1046 BCE), when the Chinese began writing. The Nian monster had a lion's head, but a large, curved horn jutted out from its forehead. It had long fangs, fiery yellow eyes, and a body like an ox or a dragon.

For most of the year, the Nian monster slept at the bottom of the sea or deep in a mountain cave. At the beginning of a new year, it came out of hibernation, hungry and looking for food. In China, the New Year falls between the end of January and the end of February—in the dead of winter. The Nian would venture into villages, breaking into their grain stores and catching chickens and dogs to eat. He would eat little children and even fully grown people if he could catch them.

Folks learned that the Nian monster disliked the color red and loud noises. The Jade Emperor even passed a law for everyone to hang red lanterns to scare the Nian away. This is why people started wearing red at the New Year and hanging red banners. They lit fireworks, banged drums, and made lots of noise to keep the Nian away from their towns and villages. They would leave food out for the Nian so it would not hurt people or animals.

One day, a monk named Hongjun Laozu (some say he was actually a god or an immortal) decided to deal with the Nian monster that was terrorizing the people. He climbed up into the mountains and found the Nian's cave.

"Nian!" he said sternly. "You must stop eating the people and scaring them!"

The Nian monster laughed. "Well, you have walked into my cave! Thank you for being my meal today."

"That won't prove anything," Laozu answered. "I'm an old man. I won't even taste good. Nor will you be able to prove your hunting skills. Are you even able to hunt? Can you catch the poisonous snakes in these mountains?"

"Of course I can!" the Nian answered. He dashed out of the cave and returned in a couple of hours. "Ha! I've eaten every poisonous snake within miles!"

"Well, that's excellent news! Thank you, Nian," the old man said, smiling. "But I have heard that many dangerous wild animals live on the back side of this mountain. Can you drive them off?"

The Nian laughed. "Easily! I'll be back soon!"

In several hours, the Nian was back. "I have chased off all the wild animals!"

"Wow! You have rid the mountains of the poisonous snakes and wild animals. Thank you!"

"You're welcome," said the Nian. "Now, I'm starving, and I shall eat you!"

"I'm old and tough and won't taste good, but you are welcome to eat me," answered Laozu. "First, let me take off my robe and tunic."

Laozu stripped down to his long underwear, which were red. "Ai ya!" screamed the Nian. He dashed away from Laozu. "Get out of my cave! Go away! I can't look at your red underwear!"

"I'm staying right here!" Laozu replied sternly. "I will get dressed again and cover my red underwear, but only if you promise not to eat people anymore."

"I promise! I promise!" the Nian screamed.

"One more thing," Laozu said. "Let me ride on your back into the village."

"Yes, yes, just don't let me see your underwear!"

Laozu got dressed, and the Nian allowed him to hop on its back. Shortly after, the people of the village looked up to see an unimaginable sight. Laozu was riding the Nian monster into town!

"It's all right," Laozu reassured the villagers. "The Nian will not hurt you. He has promised not to eat people anymore. Remember that he cannot bear the color red, so put red paper on your doors, hang red lanterns and banners, and wear red at the New Year. If you do that, he will not come near you. One more thing, he hates loud noises!"

That is why the people of China wear red at the New Year, put red paper on their doors, and hang red lanterns and banners everywhere. They set off fireworks and perform the lion dance with actors inside a lion costume moving to roaring drums and banging cymbals.

Performing the Lion Dance at New Year[30]

The Homesick Maid

Yuan Xiao was a teenage maid working in the emperor's palace during the Han dynasty. Although she knew it was an honor to work for the famous Emperor Wu, she was from a rural village and missed her family. With the Chinese New Year approaching, she grew even more homesick. This was always a time for family reunions, yet she would have to stay in the city. One day, she sat next to the well in the courtyard, remembering past New Year celebrations. Her aunts, uncles, and cousins all gathered at her grandparents' house to eat, laugh, and tell stories.

A tear traveled down Yuan Xiao's cheek. She would have to stay in the palace and work. "I wonder when I will see Mama, Baba, my brother, grandparents, and cousins again."

Dongfang Shuo walked into the courtyard. He was a court official and scholar. He was rumored to be an immortal. Yuan Xiao liked him because he had a way of making her laugh when she was feeling down. He kept the emperor and everyone else around him amused by his quick-witted wordplay and audacious truth-telling quips.

"Yuan Xiao, what's wrong? Why are you crying?"

"Oh, I'm sorry, Yuan Xiao. You've always been kind to me. Everyone here has, and I enjoy my job. It's just that I'm homesick. I miss my family. We've always been together on the New Year."

"Well, little sister, let me see what I can do. I might help you and the other palace employees see their families this New Year."

"Really? Can you do that?"

"I'm forming a plan that just might work!" Dongfang Shuo rubbed his beard.

Yuan Xiao wiped her tears. "Knowing you, it will be brilliant and clever!" She stood up and went back to work with a spring in her step.

In a few days, a coworker walked in, carrying a basket. "I just got back from the market," she said. "Guess what's happening? Dongfang Shuo is telling fortunes there!"

"Really? Well, he taught the blind men the ancient art of divination from the *I Ching* (*Book of Changes*), so they no longer have to beg. Now, they are respectable spiritual guides."

"That's right," the other maid mused. "He's always helping people. Well, anyway, he's giving everyone the same fortune. He's saying our city will go up in flames on the fifteenth day of the first lunar month! That's just next week!"

Yuan Xiao smiled to herself. She realized Dongfang Shuo was orchestrating something to her advantage.

"Has the emperor heard? What do you think he will do?" Yuan Xiao asked.

"Dongfang Shuo is the wisest man in the kingdom. I'm sure he'll give the emperor advice to prevent the disaster," the other maid said. "At least, I hope he has a plan!"

At that moment, the emperor was interrogating Dongfang Shuo about his vision and what to do.

"We need to appease the Fire God," Dongfang Shuo explained. "Have everyone make yuanxiao [rice dumplings], set off fireworks, and hang red lanterns. Order the people in the rural areas to come into the city to join in the celebration. If the Fire God sees everyone honoring him, he will be pleased, and instead of killing us, he will bless us."

The emperor sent out runners to spread the news throughout the city and in the countryside. In the palace, Yuan Xiao worked hard making yuanxiao, glutinous rice balls filled with black sesame paste and served in a sweet syrup. "This is my Nainai's recipe. My grandmother always makes the most delicious rice dumplings in our village."

"Ha ha! Did your family name you after your Nainai's dumplings?"

On the appointed day, people from the rural areas poured into the city. Fireworks exploded overhead, red lanterns lit the streets, music played, and everyone walked around greeting friends and family and enjoying yuanxiao. Dongfang Shuo guided Yuan Xiao and her coworkers through the city.

"Look at all these people! I wonder if my family is here somewhere?" Yuan Xiao mused.

Suddenly, she heard her name called. "Yuan Xiao! Yuan Xiao! Over here!"

Yuan Xiao looked across the street. "Mama! Baba! Nainai! Gege [brother]! You're all here!"

With tears streaming down her face, Yuan Xiao raced over to her family and hugged them. "I have been so homesick, but now you're all here, thanks to Dongfang Shuo! We can celebrate together as a family."

Yuan Xiao introduced her family to Dongfang Shuo and her other coworkers. As they were happily chatting, the emperor walked up. "Dongfang Shuo, I'm not sure if you were joking about the Fire God, but this is a splendid celebration. I have no doubt the Fire God is pleased, and I am also pleased. The people are all enjoying themselves, families are coming together, and it makes me happy to see them happy. We should do this Lantern Festival every year! I will pass a decree!"

The emperor smiled at Yuan Xiao. "Since this young lady makes the most delicious rice dumplings I've ever eaten, we'll name the festival after her! We'll call it the Yuan Xiao Festival!"

Roundup Activity: Thought Questions

1. The Lantern Festival is a time of joy and family. What's your favorite holiday and why?

2. If you could design your lantern for the festival, what would it look like, and what would it symbolize?

3. Yinglong fought against evil spirits to protect people. Who is someone you look up to as a protector, and why?

4. The Jade Rabbit is a symbol of selflessness. What does being selfless mean to you, and how do you show it?

5. The story of the Jade Emperor's crane portrays Heaven's supreme god as quick to anger and easily tricked. How does this imperfect god compare with deities in other cultures?

6. In the Jade Emperor's crane story, the Jade Emperor's daughter and the sage help the village escape the chief god's wrath. Do you think they did the right thing? Why or why not?

7. Hongjun Laozu confronted the problematic Nian monster by going right into its cave. What does this say about active versus passive approaches to fear and challenges?

8. The Nian legend could have simply said Hongjun Laozu wore red robes. What is the narrative effect of his red underwear? Does it add a touch of humor, vulnerability, or a surprising twist to the story?

9. Was Dongfang Shuo's deception of the emperor, by faking a threat from the fire god, justifiable to reunite Yuan Xiao with her family?

10. Aside from deceiving the emperor and the people, what does this story tell you about Dongfang Shuo's character?

Chapter 10: The Immortal Peach: The Banquet of the Gods

This last chapter relates the story of the peaches of immortality. Xi Wangmu, the Queen Mother of the West, grew these peaches in her divine orchard. Every year, she served the celestial peaches at the Feast of the Gods. The banquet and peaches symbolized eternal life and divine favor. However, one year, the rogue Monkey King crashed the party after eating the ripe peaches from Xi Wangmu's orchard. The story showcases themes of cunning, desire, and the consequences of one's actions.

Sun Wukong was not the only one stealing peaches. Dongfang Shuo, the court official who orchestrated the Lantern Festival, also stole peaches from Xi Wangmu's divine garden.

Xi Wangmu's Peaches of Immortality

The legendary peaches granted wisdom, youthfulness, and immortality to anyone who ate them. Three varieties of peaches grew in the orchard of the Jade Emperor's wife at her Jade Pool palace in the Kunlun Mountains. Heavenly dew watered her 3,600 peach trees, and the River of Stars (the Milky Way) enriched them.

The first variety of peach took three thousand years to ripen. Anyone who ate it became lighter and stronger. Their minds opened to higher wisdom, and their lives were lengthened. The second type of peach took six thousand years to mature. Those who ate it gained the ability to fly and stayed youthful, no matter their age. The third peach variety took nine thousand years to ripen and granted irreversible immortality.

Among mortals, only three people and one naughty monkey ate these celestial peaches. However, whenever any variety of the peaches ripened, Xi Wangmu threw a grand banquet for the Eight Immortals and her favorite deities.

A 19th-century silk painting of Xi Wangmu and a maid with two peaches [81]

The first person to eat a celestial peach was King Mu, who ruled the Zhou dynasty in the 10th century BCE. The *Mu Tianzi Zhuan*, a fantasy biography of Mu written in the Warring States Period (475–221 BCE), tells the story. Longing to become immortal, King Mu traveled to Mount Kunlun, which was either in the Himalayas or Heaven. He hoped to find Xi Wangmu's palace and taste one of her peaches. Since the peaches of immortality only ripened every nine thousand years, arriving at the right time would be miraculous.

Zao Fu, the king's charioteer, drove King Mu to Mount Kunlun, where Xi Wangmu hosted a banquet in his honor at the Jade Pool. They took turns reciting poetry, and the Queen Mother served bear paws, dragon liver, and monkey lips. King Mu drank heavenly wine, and for dessert, Xi Wangmu served a celestial peach. However, it must not have been the third type of peach that granted full immortality. The real-life King Mu lived for more than a century, but he eventually died.

The second person to receive the peaches of immortality, according to Chinese mythology, was Emperor Wu (156–87 BCE) of the Han dynasty. The historical Emperor Wu was a remarkable ruler who expanded China's borders to their greatest extent at the time, from Korea to central Asia. As he aged, Wu grew fascinated by immortality and gathered magicians at his court who claimed they could create pills of immortality. He climbed the five-thousand-foot-high Mount Tai and offered sacrifices to Heaven and Earth, praying to live forever.

Emperor Wu grieved the death of his favorite concubine, Li Furen, and wrote a poem in her honor:

> "The sound of her silk skirt has stopped.
>
> On the marble pavement, dust grows.
>
> Her empty room is cold and still.
>
> Fallen leaves are piled against the doors.
>
> How can I bring my aching heart to rest?"[i]

Mythology says that the goddess Xi Wangmu favored Emperor Wu so much that she visited him with seven peaches from her celestial orchard. She gave five to Wu and ate two peaches herself. The emperor ate the peaches but kept the pits so he could plant them and grow his own magical peach trees.

Xi Wangmu laughed. "It doesn't work that way. The trees bear fruit only once every three thousand years. Also, the tree will not grow in this soil. However, since you want to achieve immortality, listen carefully and follow my instructions. If you do what I tell you, then eternal life is yours."

Emperor Wu failed to follow her instructions and died when he was sixty-nine years old.

---

[i] W. Scott Morton, *China: Its History and Culture* (McGraw Hill, 1995), 54.

Dongfang Shuo Purloins Three Peaches

Dongfang Shuo was a real person; however, myths grew up around this colorful personality who served in Emperor Wu's court. When applying for a position of service to Emperor Wu, he described himself as an orphan reared by his older brother. He learned to write at twelve, studied military science, and mastered the sayings of Confucius. As an adult, he stood nearly seven feet tall.

When Xi Wangmu was visiting Emperor Wu with her gift of peaches, a movement at the window caught her eye. She frowned. "Dongfang Shuo, is that you hiding outside the Red Bird Window? Did you think I would not notice you?"

She swung around to Emperor Wu. "You should know that this man used to serve as a courtier in my palace on Mount Kunlun. He's an incarnation of the planet Jupiter. However, I banished him to live with mortals. He's not young at all, you know. He's lived for millennia."

Image from a Ming dynasty silk tapestry of Dongfang Shuo holding a peach [32]

"You banished Dongfang Shuo?" asked the emperor. "Why?"

"He stole my peaches!" Wangmu scowled. "Three times!"

"Dongfang Shuo?" asked the emperor, incredulously. "He's always been kind and helpful to everyone here. In fact, he's the funniest person I know! We call him the court jester. He always has something witty to say. Yes, he can pull some pranks, and, yes, some people think he's crazy. I think he's just eccentric. I suspect he lied about the Fire God, but he did it in good faith. He was helping someone. He has actually helped many people."

"Wonderful! I'm glad to hear that," said Xi Wangmu, smiling. "His original heart is pure. I believe he has reformed in his years here on Earth. I will allow him to return to me soon. In the meantime, treat him well!"[i]

Monkey King, the Party Crasher

This story takes place after Sun Wukong got the Ruyi Jingu Bang staff from the Dragon King but before he set off on a pilgrimage to India with Tripitaka. He had achieved partial immortality after his Taoist studies. Now, with his magical fighting rod and his supernatural kung fu skills, he was unstoppable, stirring up no end of trouble on Earth. The Jade Emperor sent his top generals down to Monkey King's mountain to arrest him. Grand Marshal Devaraja Li Jing led the celestial army.

Outside Sun Wukong's Water-Curtain Cave were tigers, wolves, and leopards. "Beasts!" snarled Li Jing's officer. "Run into the cave and tell that failed horse groom that I am here under the Jade Emperor's authority to arrest him. Tell him to come out quickly and surrender, or I will kill all of you!"

The animals ran frantically through the waterfall and into the cave, screaming, "Disaster!"

"What kind of disaster?" asked Sun Wukong.

"Heaven's army is here!" gasped the creatures. "You must surrender, or they will kill us all!"

Monkey King jumped up, put on his battle clothing, and grabbed his Ruyi Jingu Bang. He pushed through the waterfall to confront the Jade Emperor's army.

---

[i] T. E. Smith, "Ritual and the Shaping of Narrative: The Legend of the Han Emperor Wu. (Doctoral diss., University of Michigan, 1992), 416-417, ProQuest (9303824).

"Strip yourself of your armor and weapons immediately!" ordered the officer. "The Jade Emperor has ordered you to submit to me. If you utter even half a 'no,' I will kill these creatures and turn you into powder."

"Reckless fool," laughed Sun Wukong. "I could have killed you in a second, but I need you to take a message to the Jade Emperor. I possess unlimited ability. Why did he ask me to mind his horses? Read the words on my banner! If the Jade Emperor acknowledges my title, I will put down my arms, and the cosmos will be peaceful."

The officer peered at the banner, which read, "Great Sage, Equal to Heaven."

The officer laughed arrogantly. "You lawless ape! You aspire to be the Great Sage, Equal to Heaven? Take a bit of my ax first!"

He swung his ax, but Monkey King whipped out his rod and blocked it. A mighty battle ensued until Sun Wukong split the officer's battle-ax in two. The officer rushed off as Monkey King called out, "Imbecile! I spared you so you could take my message to the Jade Emperor!"

However, the officer reported back to Grand Marshal Devaraja Li Jing. At that, the Grand Marshal's son, Prince Nata, volunteered to arrest Monkey King. He dashed to Sun Wukong's cave and plunged through the waterfall.

"Whose little brother are you?" demanded Monkey King. "What do you want, barging through my gate?"

"Lawless monkey, I am here under the authority of the Jade Emperor to arrest you!"

Sun Wukong laughed. "You still have your baby teeth!"

"Swallow my sword," snarled Prince Nata.

"I'll just stand here quietly. See if you can hack me with that sword."

At that point, the enraged Prince Nata morphed into a three-headed, six-armed monster carrying six weapons.

Monkey King found this somewhat alarming. "Little brother! You do know a few tricks. Now watch *my* magic!"

He also shapeshifted into a three-headed, six-armed creature, holding three Ruyi Jingu Bangs. A mighty battle ensued that went on for thirty rounds until Sun Wukong landed a devastating blow on the prince, who hobbled back to his camp.[i]

When it became apparent that Heaven's forces could not defeat Monkey King, Grand Marshal Devaraja Li Jing reported back to the Jade Emperor.

"Blast it!" the Jade Emperor huffed. "All right. We'll give the imp his title! I'm making him the temporary guardian of the Celestial Peach Orchard. Hopefully, he'll stop his madness."

Dongfang Shuo had been the previous guardian of the Celestial Peach Orchard. However, he had been exiled for eating the peaches. Now, the post was empty, and it went to Monkey King. "No more crazy behavior!" the Jade Emperor warned.

Monkey King was delighted. He rushed to the peach orchard and met with the gardeners. "How many peach trees are here?"

"Three thousand, six hundred in all," the head gardener answered. They explained the three different types of trees and how long each variety took to produce peaches.

However, Monkey King was no better than his predecessor at protecting the peaches. When he noticed a tree with ripened peaches, he would climb up and eat the peaches to his heart's content.

Xi Wangmu had heard that some of her peaches were ripening. It was time for a celestial peach banquet! She sent her seven daughters to the peach orchard to harvest the peaches.

The princesses picked five baskets of fruit, but when they reached the back of the orchard, they found no ripe fruit on the trees. Monkey King had eaten it all! While they had been laboring, Sun Wukong had been napping in a tree. He awakened to confront the maidens. "Why are you stealing my peaches!"

"Calm yourself, Great Sage," answered the young ladies. "The Queen Mother of the West sent us to collect peaches for her banquet."

Monkey King smiled and hopped around. "Who gets invited to this banquet?"

---

[i] Cheng'en Wu, *Journey to the West*, 54-57, https://ia801307.us.archive.org/6/items/journeytothewestwuchengen1592/Journey%20to%20the%20West%20-%20Wu%20Cheng_en%201592.pdf

"Well, at the last banquet, Xi Wangmu invited the Buddha, the Bodhisattva Guanyin, the Eight Immortals, and several other distinguished guests."

"Am I invited?"

"We haven't heard our Queen Mother mention your name."

Sun Wukong scowled. He left the young women in the orchard and hurried toward Xi Wangmu's palace to sneak into the empty banquet hall. An enormous table was set with beautiful finery. Then he smelled wine! He used his magic powers to put the palace staff to sleep, and then Monkey King helped himself to the wine and delicacies. After getting thoroughly drunk, he stumbled home, but he took a wrong turn and ended up at the palace of Laozi (the founder of Taoism).

He was eager to meet Laozi, but the old gentleman was off giving a lecture. However, Monkey King found the pills of immortality and ate them. He instantly regretted his actions. "Bad! Bad!" he scolded himself. "The Jade Emperor will kill me. Wait—is that even possible? I'm immortal, especially after eating all those peaches and these pills. But I had better fly back to Earth!"[i]

The Jade Emperor was stunned to find out that Monkey King had eaten the peaches of immortality, drunk the wine meant for the banquet, and stolen Laozi's pills of immortality. And that led the Buddha to put the Monkey King into "time out" for five hundred years under a mountain.

---

[i] Cheng'en Wu, *Journey to the West*, 58-86.

Roundup Activity: Thought Questions

1. If you could eat a peach of immortality, would you? Which one would you eat and why?

2. Dongfang Shuo used his wit to get what he wanted. Can you think of a time when being funny or clever helped you?

3. Immortality is a big theme in these stories. If you were immortal, how would it change the way you live your life right now?

4. If you could be any god or mythical creature from Chinese mythology, who would you be and why?

5. Xi Wangmu's peach garden is only for gods and immortals. If you had a mythical garden, what magical things would you want in it?

6. If you could meet Xi Wangmu, the Queen Mother of the West, what would you ask her?

7. How do you think the myths of Dongfang Shuo influence how people viewed his actual life and work?

8. Despite his amazing abilities, Monkey King ruined things for himself in Heaven. What flaws in his character drove his downward spiral? Do you ever struggle with things like this?

9. Do you think being immortal could be a burden? Why or why not?

10. The Jade Emperor failed to rein in Monkey King, but the Buddha stuck him under a mountain for five centuries. If you were the parent of a rebellious teen, how would you handle the situation?

Here's another book by Enthralling History that you might like

Free limited time bonus

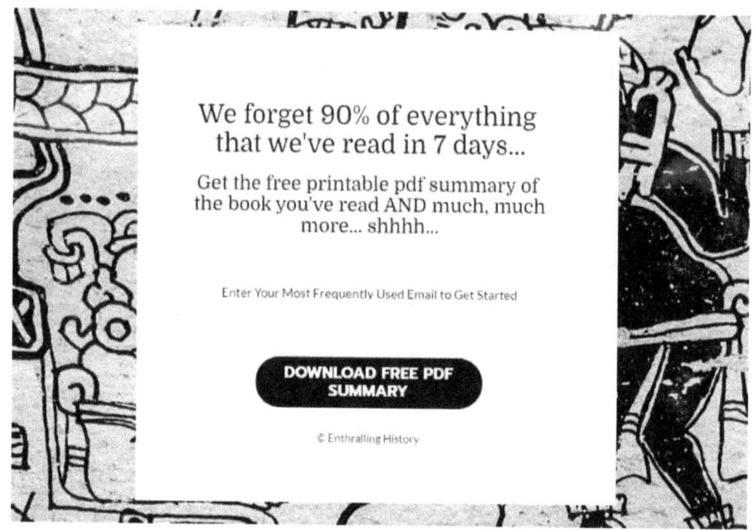

Stop for a moment. We have a free bonus set up for you. The problem is this: we forget 90% of everything that we read after 7 days. Crazy fact, right? Here's the solution: we've created a printable, 1-page pdf summary for this book that you're reading now. All you have to do to get your free pdf summary is to go to the following website:
https://livetolearn.lpages.co/enthrallinghistory/

Or, Scan the QR code!

Once you do, it will be intuitive. Enjoy, and thank you!

Bibliography

Cutter, Robert Joe. *The Poetry of Cao Zhi*. De Gruyter, 2021.

Fu, Shelley, and Patrick Yee. *Chinese Myths and Legends: The Monkey King and Other Adventures*. Tuttle Publishing, 2018.

Hamilton, Mae. "Chinese God Pangu." *Mythopedia*. Accessed July 17, 2025. https://mythopedia.com/topics/pangu/

Hamilton, Mae. "Chinese Goddess Nuwa." *Mythopedia*. Accessed July 17, 2025. https://mythopedia.com/topics/nuwa/

Huang, Dehai. *Illustrated Myths & Legends of China: The Ages of Chaos and Heroes*. Shanghai Press, 2018.

Legge, James. *The Notions of the Chinese Concerning Gods and Spirits*. Hong Kong Register, 1852.

Li Ki: Book of Rites. Translated by James Legge, 1885. Accessed July 19, 2025. https://sacred-texts.com/cfu/liki/index.htm

Ling, Vivian, Peng Wang, and Yang Xi. *A Bilingual Treasury of Chinese Folktales: Ten Traditional Stories in Chinese and English*. Tuttle Publishing, 2022.

Ling, Vivian, Peng Wang, and Yang Xi. *Chinese Stories for Language Learners: A Treasury of Proverbs and Folktales in Bilingual Chinese and English*. Tuttle Publishing, 2021.

Martens, Frederick H., and Richard Wilhelm. *Chinese Fairy Tales and Legends: A Gift Edition of Seventy-three Enchanting Chinese Folk Stories and Fairy Tales*. Bloomsbury China, 2019.

Nunes, Shiho S. and Lak-Khee Tay-Audouard. *Chinese Folktales: The Dragon Slayer and Other Timeless Tales*. Tuttle Publishing, 2021.

Scott, Morton. *China: Its History and Culture.* McGraw Hill, 1995.

Selection from the Lotus Sutra: "The Daughter of the Dragon King." Accessed August 2, 2025. Asia for Educators: Columbia University. https://afe.easia.columbia.edu/ps/cup/lotus_sutra_dragon_king.pdf

Sima Qian, *Shiji, Records of the Grand Scribe.* China Knowledge: An Encyclopedia on Chinese History and Literature. Accessed March 13, 2025. http://www.chinaknowledge.de/Literature/Historiography/shiji.html

Smith, T.E. "Ritual and the Shaping of Narrative: The Legend of the Han Emperor Wu." Doctoral diss., University of Michigan, 1992. ProQuest (9303824).

The Works of Motze. Confucius Publications, 1980.

Wilhelm, R., Norman Hinsdale Pitman, and Andrew Lang, eds. *Chinese Fairy Tales, Folktales and Fables.* Accessed July 15, 2025. https://fairytalez.com/region/chinese/#google_vignette

Wu, Cheng'en. *Journey to the West.* Accessed November 1, 2025 https://ia801307.us.archive.org/6/items/journeytothewestwuchengen1592/Journey%20to%20the%20West%20-%20Wu%20Cheng_en%201592.pdf

Wu, Qinglong, Zhijun Zhao, Li Liu, et al. "Outburst Flood at 1920 BCE Supports Historicity of China's successful Flood and the Xia Dynasty." *Science.* 353, no. 6299 (2016): 10.1126/science.aaf084 https://www.science.org/doi/10.1126/science.aaf0842

"Yellow Emperor." *China Daily.com.* March 12, 2012. Accessed July 17, 2008. https://www.chinadaily.com.cn/life/yellow_emperor_memorial_ceremony/2012-03/12/content_14812971.htm

Image Sources

1 Internet Archive Book Images, No restrictions, via Wikimedia Commons; https://commons.wikimedia.org/wiki/File:The_dragon,_image,_and_demon;_or,_T he_three_religions_of_China-_Confucianism,_Buddhism,_and_Taoism,_ giving_an_account_of_the_mythology,_idolatry,_and_demonolatry_of_the_Chinese _(1887)_(14783597882).jpg

2 Credit: BabelStone, CC BY-SA 3.0 <https://creativecommons.org/licenses/by-sa/3.0>, via Wikimedia Commons: https://commons.wikimedia.org/wiki/File: Oracle_bones_at_Pitt_Rivers_Museum.jpg

3 https://commons.wikimedia.org/wiki/File:Twelve_Symbols_national_ emblem_of_China.svg

4 User:Vmenkov, CC BY-SA 3.0 <https://creativecommons.org/licenses/by-sa/3.0>, via Wikimedia Commons: https://commons.wikimedia.org/wiki/File:Xiao_Xiu_- _NE_turtle_-_P1070560.JPG

5 https://commons.wikimedia.org/wiki/File:Shanhaijing_N%C3%BCwa_ Mends_the_Heavens.svg

6 https://commons.wikimedia.org/wiki/File:Anonymous-Fuxi_and_N%C3%BCwa.jpg

7 https://commons.wikimedia.org/wiki/File:Yellow_Emperor.jpg#file

8 https://commons.wikimedia.org/wiki/File:Court_ladies_pounding_silk_ from_a_painting_(%E6%8D%A3%E7%BB%83%E5%9B%BE)_by_Emperor_Huiz ong.jpg

9 https://commons.wikimedia.org/wiki/File:Confucius,_fresco_from_a_ Western_Han_tomb_of_Dongping_County,_Shandong_province,_China.jpg

10 Windmemories, CC BY-SA 4.0 <https://creativecommons.org/licenses/by-sa/4.0>, via Wikimedia Commons: https://commons.wikimedia.org/wiki/File: 20230108_Statue_of_Jiang_Ziya_at_Weihe_Park.jpg

11 https://commons.wikimedia.org/wiki/File:Hue-EightImmortals.JPG

12 https://commons.wikimedia.org/wiki/File:Eight_Immortals_Crossing_the_Sea_- _Project_Gutenberg_eText_15250.jpg

13 https://commons.wikimedia.org/wiki/File:Album_of_18_Daoist_Paintings_-_10.jpg

14 https://commons.wikimedia.org/wiki/File:La_expedici%C3%B3n_de_Xu_ Fu,_por_Utagawa_Kuniyoshi.jpg

15 https://commons.wikimedia.org/wiki/File:Xian_guerreros_terracota_detalle.JPG

16 https://commons.wikimedia.org/wiki/File:Niulang_and_Zhinv_ (Long_Corridor).JPG

17 https://commons.wikimedia.org/wiki/File:Chang%27e_flies_to_the_moon_- _Project_Gutenberg_eText_15250.jpg

18 Huangdan2060, CC0, via Wikimedia Commons: https://commons.wikimedia.org/wiki/File:Statue_in_Yueyang,_Hunan,_China.jpg

19 Etching by Anonymous (Minor file corrections by User:Shibo77), Public domain, via Wikimedia Commons: https://commons.wikimedia.org/wiki/File:%E5%90% 8E%E7%BE%BF%E5%B0%84%E6%97%A5.png

20 Photo zoomed in. Source: Xiao Yuncong, Public domain, via Wikimedia Commons: https://commons.wikimedia.org/wiki/File:Li_sao_ illustr%C3%A9_4_21.png

21 https://commons.wikimedia.org/wiki/File:Pair_of_Bowls_(Wan)_with_ Dragons_Chasing_Flaming_Pearl_LACMA_58.51.2a-b_(2_of_4).jpg

22 Metropolitan Museum of Art, CC0, via Wikimedia Commons:https://commons.wikimedia.org/wiki/File:MET_TR.457.2012_image000 2_(Moving_Chinese_dragon).jpg

23 deror_avi, CC BY-SA 3.0 <https://creativecommons.org/licenses/by-sa/3.0>, via Wikimedia Commons: https://commons.wikimedia.org/wiki/File: Dragon_and_Phoenix_IMG_5045.jpg

24 https://commons.wikimedia.org/wiki/File:1962- 01_1962%E5%B9%B4_%E6%B5%99%E6%B1%9F%E7%BB%8D%E5%89%A7_ %E5%AD%99%E6%82%9F%E7%A9%BA.jpg

25 d'n'c from Beijing, CC BY-SA 2.0 <https://creativecommons.org/licenses/by-sa/2.0>, via Wikimedia Commons: https://commons.wikimedia.org/wiki/File: Sun_Wukong_at_Beijing_opera_-_Journey_to_the_West.jpg

26 https://commons.wikimedia.org/wiki/File:Xuanzang_w.jpg

27 This file is licensed under the Creative Commons Attribution-Share Alike 3.0 Unported license.: CC BY-SA 3.0 <https://creativecommons.org/licenses/by-

sa/3.0/deed.en > https://commons.wikimedia.org/wiki/File:
JourneytotheWest.jpg#file

28 https://commons.wikimedia.org/wiki/File:Statue_at_Wuhan_Da_Yu_
Cultural_Garden_2017.jpeg#file

29 Silentpilot, CC0, via Wikimedia Commons:
https://commons.wikimedia.org/wiki/File:Red-lantern-1202514.jpg

30 https://commons.wikimedia.org/wiki/File:Lion_dance2015.jpg

31 Sotheby's, lot.12, Public domain, via Wikimedia Commons:
https://commons.wikimedia.org/wiki/File:Yu_Zhiding_-
_Xi_Wangmu_(The_Queen_Mother_of_the_West).jpg

32 https://commons.wikimedia.org/wiki/File:The_Immortal_Dongfang_
Shuo_Stealing_a_Peach,_close-up_of_tapestry.jpg

www.ingramcontent.com/pod-product-compliance
Lightning Source LLC
Chambersburg PA
CBHW050752150726

48196CB00004B/444